Palestinian Democracy and Governance

An Appraisal of the Legislative Council

David Schenker

Policy Papers no. 51

THE WASHINGTON INSTITUTE FOR NEAR EAST POLICY

Published in 2000 in the United States of America by the Washington Institute for Near East Policy, 1828 L Street NW, Suite 1050, Washington, DC 20036.

Library of Congress Cataloging-in-Publication Data

Schenker, David Kenneth, 1968–
Palestinian Democracy and Governance: an appraisal of the Legislative Council / David Schenker.
p. cm. — (Policy papers ; no. 51)
Includes bibliographical references (p.).
ISBN 0-944029-34-5 (pbk.)
1. Palestinian National Authority. Majlis al-Tashrå°'. 2. Palestinian Arabs—Politics and government. 3. Arab–Israeli conflict—1993—Peace. I. Title. II. Policy papers (Washington Institute for Near East Policy) ; no. 51.
JQ1830.A71 P3537 1999
328.5695'3—dc21 99-054846
CIP

Cover photo © Corbis.
Cover design by Monica Neal Hertzman.

The Author

David K. Schenker is a research fellow at The Washington Institute for Near East Policy specializing in Arab politics and terrorism. He joined the Institute in August 1998.

From 1997 to 1998, Mr. Schenker was Senior Researcher at the Investigative Project, where he analyzed Middle Eastern terrorist organizations and U.S. counter-terrorism policy. From 1994 to 1996, he worked for a private contractor, managing USAID projects in Egypt and Jordan. During that time, Mr. Schenker was also a consultant on Middle Eastern affairs for the Department of Defense.

Mr. Schenker received his B.A. in Political Science in 1990 from the University of Vermont and his M.A. in Modern Middle Eastern Studies in 1992 from the University of Michigan. From 1992 to 1993 he studied Arabic in Egypt while on a CASA Fellowship. Most recently, Mr. Schenker is the author of "The Palestinian Authority: A Hybrid Creation," in *Middle East Quarterly* (September 1999).

• • •

Table of Contents

Acknowledgments		vii
Preface		ix
Executive Summary		xi
1	Introduction	1
2	The Structure of the Palestinian Legislative Council	7
3	Imbalance in Governance: Executive Authority and the Oversight Role of the PLC	23
4	The PLC and Internal Palestinian Governance	49
5	The PLC and the Peace Process	83
6	Israel, the United States, and the PLC	99
7	Conclusion	117

Appendices

I	PLC Candidate and Member Affiliation	125
II	Procedural Path of Draft Law (Bill) in the PLC	126
III	PLC Committee Work Schedule	128
IV	Translation of a PLC Resolution	129
V	Laws Proposed and Passed by the PLC	130
VI	Memorandum of Understanding	136

Acknowledgments

I am deeply indebted to the many people—Arabs, Israelis, and Americans—who assisted me with this study. Given the current nature of the Palestinian Authority, discretion prevents me from thanking the Palestinians I interviewed: Some of those who informed this paper have subsequently (though not consequently) been jailed or beaten. Many Palestinians I spoke with are strong advocates for democratization in the PA. I thank these interviewees for their help, and wish them the best of luck in their quest for good governance.

In Washington, my perspective has to some extent been guided by discussions with analysts and scholars. In particular, I thank Harold Rhode, David Wurmser, Azar Nafisi and Abbas Kelidar; in addition to being colleagues and mentors, they are valued friends.

For the past year and a half, I have had the good fortune to work in an environment where I've been afforded great independence and encouraged to research and write. For this and his significant contribution to this study, I am extremely grateful to Robert Satloff, executive director of The Washington Institute. The paper also benefitted from the careful readings of my Institute colleagues Patrick Clawson, Alan Makovsky, and Adiba Mango. Forsan Hussein, a summer intern at the Institute, provided helpful research assistance, and the Publications staff, Monica Neal Hertzman and Alicia Gansz, were patient, professional, and a pleasure to work with from start to finish.

I'd also like to thank my family, which has been a consistent source of support and happiness. In this regard, I consider myself quite fortunate.

• • •

While the insights I gained from my interviews and colleagues were invaluable to this paper, I alone bear responsibility for its content and deficiencies. Translations from Arabic are mine, unless otherwise noted.

Preface

Democratization has long been a poor cousin to Arab–Israeli peacemaking and Gulf security in the list of U.S. policy priorities in the Middle East. Every year, Washington spends millions of dollars to promote democracy in the Middle East, and it is one of several elements in a U.S. foreign assistance package to the Palestinian Authority (PA). Yet, rarely, if ever, has presidential attention or urgency been devoted to the cause of democratization in this region of the world, even though the linkage between peace and democracy seems intuitive.

Indeed, Palestinian governance is a topic that is often discussed, but seldom with regard to the peace process. In Washington, as in Jerusalem, the overriding concerns on the Palestinian track have been based on security. But even in this context, far too little attention has been devoted to the authoritarian state-in-the-making in the West Bank and Gaza and its implications for the sustainability of peace between Israelis and Palestinians. The analytical questions at the heart of the issue are: Would a democratic PA be better or worse for the peace process? Just how important is democracy to a lasting peace between Israel and the Palestinians? And how important are the Palestinians as a model for other Arab states in the region, many of whom are facing regime changes and uncertain futures?

In this study, David Schenker, a research fellow of Arab politics at The Washington Institute, provides an assessment of Palestinian governance and its impact on peace by looking through the prism of the Palestinian Legislative Council (PLC), the legislative branch of government in the Palestinian Authority. He describes the origin and development of the PLC, its legislative and oversight roles, as well as the legislature's relationship to the executive authority headed by Yasir Arafat. Mr. Schenker's analysis also focuses on the implications of the PLC's performance for the peace process and for the future of Palestinian governance.

The PLC, he argues, is the bellwether of democracy in the PA. Although the PLC has often proven to be a complicating factor in the Israeli–Palestinian peace process, Mr. Schenker nevertheless points out that it has the potential to be the driving force for good governance and accountability in the PA. In the long run, he says, this could contribute to a more stable PA and a better neighbor for Israel.

As Israelis and Palestinians move closer to a "permanent status agreement," their peace will be defined more and more by the quality of their relationship, not just the termination of conflict. The extent to which an Arab democracy evolves to live side by side with Israel's democracy will be crucial. We present Mr. Schenker's path-breaking study in the hope not only that it will provoke debate on a highly sensitive yet vitally important issue, but also that it will prod American policymakers to consider new and creative ways to invest in the long-term potential for democratization in the Palestinian Authority.

Michael Stein
Chairman

Fred S. Lafer
President

Executive Summary

Democracy and governance in the Middle East has become a hot topic in Washington. Policymakers who have traditionally focused on the Arab–Israeli peace process have started to take a hard look at the role that democracy and (good) governance can play in maintaining peace in the region. Nowhere is this issue more crucial than in the Palestinian Authority (PA). Nearly five years into the experiment of self-rule, Palestinian politics is at the crossroads of democracy and dictatorship. It is unlikely, but not inconceivable, that the PA will become the first full-fledged Arab democracy. The direction in which Palestinian governance proceeds will necessarily have an effect on the peace process.

Background

On January 20, 1996, residents of the PA went to the polls to vote for their provisional government. In addition to electing longtime Palestine Liberation Organization (PLO) leader Yasir Arafat as *ra'is* (president), Palestinians elected eighty-eight district representatives to the *Majlis al-Tashre'i*—the Palestinian Legislative Council (PLC).

Originally conceived in the 1993 Oslo Declaration of Principles between Israel and the PLO, the PLC is an institution mandated in the text of several Israeli–Palestinian agreements, including the 1994 Agreement on the Gaza Strip and Jericho Area and the 1995 Israeli–Palestinian Interim Agreement on the West Bank and the Gaza Strip (Oslo II). But the central role technically afforded to the PLC in Palestinian governance—that of legislating and providing oversight to the executive authority—has yet to materialize. Despite high expectations and promising beginnings, the PLC has failed to carve out a meaningful and significant role in the Palestinian political arena. Beset by both internal and external problems, the Palestinian legislature has become a peripheral institution, which does not bode well for the future of good governance in the PA.

Legislative Endeavors

In general terms, PLC efforts can be classified as belonging to two categories: activities related to governance, and activities related to the peace process. Contrary to popular perception, most of the PLC's efforts are directly related to the former. In its first three years, the PLC worked on a broad spectrum of governance laws, including budgets, civil service reforms, regulation of natural resources, and a law ensuring protection of the disabled in the PA. In terms of peace process–related legislation, the PLC worked on a law prohibiting the sale of real estate to foreigners as well as a law mandating national service. All told, between January 1996 and October 1999, the PLC worked on over sixty laws, about twenty-five of which were passed. Only six or seven of these laws were even remotely peace process–related

To take on the force of law in the PA, draft laws passed by the PLC should be ratified by Ra'is Arafat, but in any event they must be published in the *Official Gazette.* As of February 1999, Arafat had ratified only sixteen of the twenty-five laws the PLC had passed; by October, he had ratified twenty of the twenty-six laws—and only two of them were related to the peace process. The most conspicuous and bitterly contested of the unratified laws is the Basic Law—the Palestinian Constitution—which was referred to Arafat for ratification in April 1997. The legislative history of the Basic Law typifies the experience of the PLC and particularly the dynamic between the legislative and executive authorities of the PA. Indeed, Arafat's refusal to ratify this law set a bad precedent that has been repeated with great regularity. Since the PLC's establishment, Arafat has ignored the council and its legislation with impunity.

Problems with the Executive

To a large extent, problems of the PLC stem from the fact that the PA is an authoritarian rather than a democratic entity. While the PA ostensibly possesses the architecture of a democracy, power in Palestinian politics has from the very beginning gravitated toward Arafat's executive authority. Moreover, because most of the members of the legislature are also loyal members of Fatah—the wing of the PLO that Arafat most directly controls—there is little willingness in the PLC to oppose executive dictate. This problem is further exacerbated by the fact that the PLC's Speaker, its top officers, and leading administrators are strong supporters and benefactors of the ra'is.

As with other parliaments, the PLC does possess a number of methods to censure, embarrass, or otherwise pressure the executive. The Palestinian legislature can employ votes of no confidence to threaten or remove uncooperative ministers, executive authority officials, or even the ra'is himself. The PLC can also initiate oversight procedures, such as public hearings, to debate issues and investigate executive authority policies. Given the composition of the legislature, however, it is not surprising that, despite numerous threats to do so, it has never employed a vote of no confidence against Arafat or his cabinet. By not following through on its threats, the PLC has undermined its own authority and enforced the popular perception that it is an institutional paper tiger.

The PLC, Israel, and U.S. Policy

One of the main criticisms leveled against the PLC is that it is preoccupied with—and plays a counterproductive role in—the peace process. Many Israeli and American policymakers subscribe to this point of view and advocate the continuation of Arafat's dominant position vis-à-vis the legislature. Not surprisingly, Israeli concerns regarding the PA are primarily, and perhaps solely, related to security issues. Although some Israeli officials express displeasure with specific PLC laws—those which contravene previously existing agreements—Israeli officials have for the most part not been particularly interested in the nature of Palestinian governance. Israel supports a PA that can fight Islamic militancy and terrorism, regardless of its stance on human rights and due process.

In Washington, policy toward the PA is largely guided by peace process concerns. Based on these concerns, Washington has been a consistent supporter of Arafat, who Americans believe can "deliver" the peace. At the same time, the United States has generally failed to support what may be the sole democratic public institution in the PA—the Palestinian Legislative Council. Although this policy may ensure continuity and incremental progress in the peace process, it does not take into account the established link between peace and democracy. Despite the intuitive connection between the two, democracy has rarely if ever been a topic of discussion related to the peace process.

In terms of the Palestinians, however, it should be. In the PA—where the population has both a knowledge of and an appreciation for democracy—the discussion is timely and relevant. Unlike many of the peoples of the region, Palestinians have a history in which participation, pluralism, and respect for rule of law are not alien concepts. Given the proper circumstances, and the requisite encouragement from the United States, these factors could facilitate the development of a more democratic PA. Such a transformation will likely be necessary for the Palestinians to reach an acceptable and popularly supported peace with the Israelis. Moreover, democracy will be an element essential to sustain and strengthen any agreement reached between the parties.

The PLC—which possesses a legitimacy unmatched by any other branch of the PA—can play a key role in democratic development and in furthering the peace process with Israel. Contrary to the prevailing wisdom, there is no indication that a strong PLC would be any more problematic than Arafat is in terms of movement on the peace process. In fact, although a more robust PLC might initially complicate the process, in the long term it would almost certainly ensure a more accountable PA. More accountability would generate more consistent financial support from the international donor community, attract more foreign investment in the Palestinian economy, and inspire more confidence and political moderation in the PA. In short, a more prominent role for the PLC would promote a more stable Palestinian neighbor, one which would likely feel more comfortable and secure in making the type of concessions and difficult political decisions necessary to ensure a real peace with Israel.

Although the United States is not reconsidering its support for Arafat, it is also keeping one foot in the democratization door by providing several million dollars to the PLC via a few projects in Ramallah funded by the U.S. Agency for International Development (USAID). But given the current status of the PLC and the general state of democracy in the PA, cash alone may not be enough. In addition to the steady provision of financial assistance to democratization and governance projects in the PA, it is imperative that the United States institute more high-level official contacts with the PLC so as to strengthen the legislative branch in the coming years. Likewise, Washington should emit a consistent message encouraging the nascent Palestinian democracy, which includes, among other things, decisive support for both legislative and local council elections in the PA. Finally, U.S. democratization programs in the PA should break from past tradition and push initiatives that focus on human rights and financial transparency. In the past, these types of initiatives have been shunned by high-ranking Arafat supporters within the PLC.

In the short run, Israeli–Palestinian peace will be based on treaties. In the long run, however, these alone are unlikely to sustain the peace. More than anything else, a lasting peace between Israelis and Palestinians will depend on the existence of a transparent, accountable democratic Palestinian government. As the PA moves toward statehood, and as the Israelis and Palestinians move toward peace, the PLC could very well provide the necessary foundation required for good Palestinian governance. Democracies, it would seem, tend to make for better neighbors

Chapter 1

Introduction

"Democratization" is once again a hot topic among Washington policymakers, analysts, and academics dealing with Middle Eastern affairs. Ongoing discussions about political participation and governmental accountability concern the gamut of Middle East states, from the new generation of "liberalizing monarchies" in Jordan and Morocco to the "hereditary republics" of Syria and, potentially, Libya.[1] Among the states and entities under evaluation, however, few have received as much attention as the Palestinian Authority (PA).

In its relatively short history, Palestinian governance has been the subject of several high-profile studies, critiques, and assessments.[2] It is as if a large magnifying glass has been focused on the institutions of Palestinian government. The intense interest in the PA is clearly related to the peace process and the prospects for a sustainable regional peace. But it also seems apparent that this focus on Palestinian governance is attributable to the fact that Palestinians are, in many ways, unique among their Arab neighbors. Unlike the Gulf dynasties, the Islamic states, or the various authoritarian republics and monarchies in the region, it is conceivable that, in the near future, the PA could become a democracy.

The direction in which Palestinian governance evolves—either toward democracy or toward dictatorship—will depend on the development of PA institutions. Among these institutions, one of the more important ones is the Palestinian Legislative Council (PLC), the subject of this study. Since its establishment in 1996, the popularly elected PLC has often been dismissed as an ineffective and irrelevant organization or, worse, as a rubber-stamp parliament. To be sure, the PLC has operated under difficult circumstances, and has not realized its potential. Despite missed opportunities in its initial years, however, the PLC is in a unique position in the Palestinian political arena. It is the only Palestinian institution with the tools at its disposal to ensure good governance in the PA.

Perhaps the inefficacy of the PLC was to be expected. After all, the PA is in its infancy, and it would be unrealistic to expect an immature institution such as the PLC to vie for power on a level playing field with a political veteran like Yasir Arafat, the longtime Palestine Liberation Organization (PLO) chairman and PA *ra'is* (president). Even so, the pattern of interaction between the legislature and the chief executive does not appear to be moving toward a compromise or any type of equilibrium. In many ways, the legislative council's frustrated efforts are indicative of the overall state of democratic development in the PA.

It is rather ironic that Palestinian governance is so problematic. With the exception of the Lebanese, Palestinians are perhaps the only Arabs to enjoy a heritage infused with democratic tradition. Indeed, relatively speaking, the Palestinians have a rich democratic legacy—one that is shared by West Bankers and Gazans as well as by the sizable Palestinian diaspora community. Even the PLO—the revolutionary umbrella organization created in 1964—is ostensibly a pluralistic and inclusive organization.

The roots of Palestinian democratic experience in the West Bank and Gaza lie in the historically vibrant civil society, the nonreligious realm of institutions in which the "mainsprings of organization, initiative, and action come from within the society rather than from above."[3] For Palestinians, this sector consists of nongovernmental organizations (NGOs) including charities, professional associations, trade unions, women's organizations, student groups, and other associations. Many studies maintain that these autonomous organizations provide a counterbalance to the power of the state, both by encouraging pluralism and by establishing an organizational framework for articulating group interests.[4] In short, these groups provide a cornerstone for democratic development.

In addition to the indirect role NGOs have played in encouraging democracy, Palestinians have also had direct experience with democracy. Many NGOs themselves—such as student councils and professional unions—are governed by democratic principles. Palestinians vote for union leaders and participate in student council elections. In 1972 and 1976, while still under Israeli occupation, West Bank Palestinians participated in direct elections for their *baladiyya* (municipal) representatives, including town councils and mayoralties.

Living under occupation for nearly thirty years, during which time they watched Israeli television and listened to Israeli radio, Palestinians have also gained an intimate knowledge of Israeli democracy. Regardless of how they feel about Israel and Israelis, Palestinians express a keen appreciation for Israeli democracy and have repeatedly stated in their public opinion polls a desire to emulate the Israeli system.[5] Palestinians in the West Bank and Gaza know what democracy is: They respect it and crave it. Likewise, those members of the Palestinian diaspora who have lived for years in the West are also well acquainted with democratic practices and principles.

In contrast to the robust civil society of the rank-and-file Palestinians in the West Bank and Gaza, the longtime Palestinian leadership—the PLO—is an inclusive, but not democratic, organization. PLO leaders have historically been supportive of party pluralism and have long engaged in the discourse of democracy, but since the organization's establishment in 1964, there have been few accompanying signs of democratic practices. From the beginning, Arafat and his dominant Fatah party sought to keep divergent parties within the larger PLO umbrella and maintain a degree of group consensus. The "national dialogue" that resulted in the 1999 rapprochement between Fatah and George Habash's Popular Front for the Liberation of Palestine (PFLP) was, in a sense, merely the latest twist in a discussion that began in 1968.

Pluralism, however, is not democracy. And despite the democratic trappings of Palestinian National Council (PNC) meetings, the PLO is not, in nature or practice, a democracy. It is a nepotistic and autocratic institution in which loyalty is valued above all else. This organization's failings were perhaps best summarized by Palestinian political scientist and PLC member Ziad Abu-Amr, who said, "There is no tradition of accountability in the Palestinian national movement."[6] The PLO is a Third World liberation organization with a revolutionary mindset—a mindset that is not particularly compatible with, or appropriate for, governing an emerging state.

This dichotomy and the challenge it poses to the PLO—which inherited the mantle of Palestinian government—was recognized in 1993 following the signing of the Oslo Declaration of Principles. At that time, Jamil Hilal, then director of the PLO Information Department in Tunis, wrote that, given the new circumstances, the PLO "has no option but to reconstruct itself to give more weight to its representative and democratic functions."[7]

The PLO began its transition to state building when the PA was established in 1994. Given that Palestinians have generally benefited from high levels of education, an advanced civil society, and exposure to democracy, the various Palestinian constituencies had high expectations for their nascent government. It was hoped that the indigenous Palestinian advocates of democracy would be able to overcome the autocrats in the ranks of the PLO bureaucracy in exile and that the PA would acquire fundamentally democratic characteristics. Although it remains to be seen whether a democracy will ultimately emerge, the short-term evidence does not inspire optimism.

Yes, state building is taking place. But, to a large extent, this process appears to be solidifying the preeminent position of Fatah in a single-party Palestinian state. There are few indications to suggest that the PLO is modifying itself from a revolutionary organization to an efficient, modern government. Appropriate institutions have been created—a legislature and a judiciary—but these institutions remain ineffective, powerless to oppose the will of the weighty executive authority. Structural barriers render the legislature and the judiciary incapable of performing the tasks for which they were created. Notwithstanding the establishment of the PA, the Fatah faction of the PLO continues to dominate the Palestinian political landscape.

The single-party system has serious repercussions for those who would advocate democratic reform. In the PA, Fatah's political opponents are perceived as "enemies," and treated as such. Criticizing Arafat and Fatah is routinely met with "crackdowns" and arrests. Civil society institutions are viewed with suspicion. Internal and external "threats" to the security of the PA remain a primary justification for Fatah's continued autocratic behavior. Domestically, the threat is attributed to Islamists; externally, it is ascribed to the Israelis.

The PA's strong authoritarian tendencies have been a source of great disappointment to many Palestinians, in part because the Palestinians had expected so much. There is no doubt that democratization takes time, but the prevalent perception that the PA is not progressing toward good governance is causing many Palestinians to despair. They comprehend the significance of their democratic tradition and sense the historic opportunity before them; moreover, they recognize that the quality of their government *now* is setting the precedent for Palestinian governance in the future.

The PLC, more than any other PA institution, is representative of pro-democracy forces. As goes the PLC, one might say, so goes Palestinian democracy. The success or failure of the PLC could have far-reaching consequences. An effective Palestinian legislature could be an integral element of a democratic Palestinian state, a source of moderation and regional stability. But if this scenario is to materialize, the PLC must evolve into a powerful institution.

This paper is an attempt to provide an understanding of what the PLC does and of the types of challenges it faces while trying to carry out its legally mandated role of legislating and providing oversight to the executive authority. Until recently, the legislative council had not received much attention by those focusing on Palestinian politics. The PLC merits a closer look, however, not only because of its importance to Palestinian governance, but also because of its role in the peace process.

Notes

1. Many Arabs refer derisively to "hereditary republics" like Egypt's as "*jamlakiyya*"—a hybrid of "*jumhurriyya*" (republic) and "*mamlaka*" (kingdom).

2. See the 1999 Independent Task Force Report, *Strengthening Palestinian Public Institutions* (New York: Council on Foreign Relations, 1999); *The Palestinian Legislative Council: An Evaluation of Its Activities During Its Third Session* (in Arabic) (Gaza City: *al-Markaz al-Falastini li-huquq al-'Insan* [Palestinian Center for Human Rights (PCHR)], 1999); among others.

3. Bernard Lewis, "State and Society under Islam," *Wilson Quarterly* 13, no. 4 (Autumn 1989).

4. Bagat Korany, Rex Brynen, and Paul Noble, *Political Liberalization and Democratization in the Arab World*, vol. 2 (Boulder, Colo.: Lynne Rienner, 1999), p. 273.

5. See for example, Center for Palestine Research and Studies (CPRS), *Palestinian Public Opinion Poll no. 39*, January 1999. Palestinians routinely say that Israeli democracy is preferable to American democracy.

6. Ziad Abu-Amr, "Pluralism and the Palestinians," *Journal of Democracy* 7, no. 3 (1996).

7. Jamil Hilal, "PLO Institutions: The Challenge Ahead," *Journal of Palestine Studies* 23, no. 1 (Autumn 1993), pp. 46–60.

Chapter 2

The Structure of the Palestinian Legislative Council

In the postelection euphoria of 1996, newly elected Palestinian legislators embarked on the difficult task of establishing their legislature from the ground up. This endeavor was virgin territory for the Palestinians, a dramatic shift from the nearly three decades of Third World "liberation organization" politics that had, until then, characterized the Palestinian political sphere. Still, in this difficult transition, the Palestinians were not without direction. The Oslo accords provided detailed guidance regarding the recommended form and function of the "Palestinian Council"—its structure, its powers, and its role in Palestinian governance.[1]

To a large extent, the Palestinian Council—which has come to be known as the Palestinian Legislative Council (PLC)—was constructed in accordance with the provided guidelines and has evolved to take on the appearance of a functioning democratic legislature. From a structural standpoint, the PLC's regulations and operating procedures are adequate, if not exemplary. In the PA—which is characterized by its bureaucratic inefficiencies—the PLC is distinguished by its relative institutional competence. Although it is immature in form, the legislature is rapidly developing into an impressive organization. Of course, this fact bears little relation to the amount of power that the legislature actually wields in the PA (this topic will be the focus of chapter three). With continued U.S. government technical assistance, however, the systems and organization of the PLC will only improve.

Roots of the Palestinian Legislative Council

The PLC was conceived in the Declaration of Principles on Interim Self-Government Arrangements (known as the DOP or Oslo I), which the Palestine Liberation Organization (PLO) and the government of Israel signed on September 13, 1993. Article I of the DOP specifies that the "aim of the Israeli–Palestinian negotiations . . . is, among other things, to establish a Palestinian Interim Self-Government Authority, *the elected Council*"(emphasis added). According to the DOP, the "Palestinian Council," once elected and operational, would itself constitute the Palestinian interim government writ large, not just a legislative branch of government.

The Palestinian Council was again mentioned in the Agreement on the Gaza Strip and the Jericho Area, which was signed in Cairo on May 4, 1994. This agreement set the parameters for the first Israeli withdrawal from territories transferred to the Palestinians. Because the Palestinian Council would not be immediately operational—elections first needed to be held—the Gaza–Jericho agreement established the "Palestinian Authority," a twenty-four–member organization "responsible for all the legislative and executive powers." The agreement stipulated that, "pending the inauguration of the Council," the offices of the Palestinian Authority (PA) would be located in the Gaza Strip and Jericho Area.

Oslo II, the 315-page agreement signed by Israel and the PLO on September 28, 1995, known formally as the Palestinian–Israeli Interim Agreement on the West Bank and the Gaza Strip, provided the most detailed description of the composition of the Palestinian Council and its role in Palestinian governance. According to this agreement, the council would consist of eighty-two members plus a *ra'is* (president) of the council's executive authority.[2] Both the council and the ra'is would be directly elected by Palestinians in the West Bank, Gaza, and Jerusalem. Article V of the Interim Agreement defined the executive as a committee within the council that would exercise executive authority on the council's behalf. The ra'is would be an *ex officio* member of this executive.

The majority of executive authority members would also be members of the council, selected by the ra'is and endorsed by the council itself. According to the agreement, the council's authority would encompass all matters within its territorial jurisdiction except for issues to be negotiated in the permanent status negotiations: Jerusalem, settlements, specified military locations, Palestinian refugees, borders, and foreign relations.

Oslo II assigned to the Palestinian Council specific legislative, executive, and judicial powers and responsibilities. In addition to the power to adopt legislation, the council was tasked with establishing "an independent judicial system composed of independent Palestinian courts and tribunals."[3] The ra'is was also authorized to initiate legislation, promulgate legislation adopted by the council, and issue secondary legislation relating to matters touching on primary legislation adopted by the council. In addition to its legislative duties, the council was assigned responsibilities related to security arrangements—including the areas of civil affairs, maintaining public order, and providing internal security. Article XIV of the Interim Agreement also authorized the council to establish a "strong police force."

Oslo II placed restrictions on the powers and jurisdiction of the council as well. The agreement stated, for example, that the council would not have "powers and responsibilities in the sphere of foreign relations." According to paragraph 4(a) of Article XVIII:

> Legislation, including legislation which amends or abrogates existing laws or military orders, which exceeds the jurisdiction of the Council or which is otherwise inconsistent with the provisions of the DOP, this Agreement, or of any other agreement that may be reached between the two sides during the interim period, shall have no effect and shall be void *ab initio* [from the beginning].

In short, any legislation passed by the council inconsistent with Palestinian commitments made to Israel would be automatically null and void. Likewise, paragraph 4(b) specified that the ra'is of the executive authority should not "promulgate legislation adopted by the Council if such legislation falls under the provisions" of the above-mentioned clause. A joint Israeli–Palestinian legal committee was designated to discuss any legislation to which Israel considered the provisions of paragraph 4(b) to apply.

Elections

Oslo II also discussed the subject of elections. Article II of Chapter 1 mandated that "direct, free" political elections would be held so Palestinians "may govern themselves according to democratic principles."[4] Article II, paragraph 2, stated that the intent of the elections was to "provide a democratic basis for the establishment of Palestinian institutions." The first Palestinian elections to elect the ra'is and members of the Palestinian Council were to take place at the "earliest practicable date" following the Israeli redeployment.

After nearly five months of preparation, on January 20, 1996, Palestinians in the West Bank and Gaza Strip went to the polls. Six hundred and seventy-two candidates campaigned for the eighty-eight available seats in the PLC.[5] Two thousand international observers watched as 75 percent of registered Palestinian voters participated in what by most accounts were free and fair elections. Balloting was carried out according to a multiple vote, multidistrict system—voters had the same number of ballots as there were seats in their district, but they could cast only one vote per candidate. In some districts, a specific number of seats were allocated to Christians to ensure religious diversity in representation.[6] According to official Palestinian statistics, Fatah candidates took fifty seats and independents thirty-five; the National Democratic Party, the Liberty and Independence Bloc, and FIDA, the Democratic Palestine Party—an offshoot of the Democratic Front for the Liberation of Palestine, or DFLP—each took one seat. (See Appendix I.)

These stated affiliations, however, do not necessarily provide an accurate picture of the political loyalties of the candidates. According to information subsequently provided by the candidates, the postelection stated political affiliations of the eighty-eight members were as follows: Fatah, sixty-four seats; independents, seventeen; Islamist candidates, six; and the People's Front for the Liberation of Palestine (PFLP), one. (See Appendix I.) The Islamist parties—Hamas and the Palestinian Islamic Jihad—as well as other opposition parties boycotted the elections and have no formal party representation in the council.[7]

The PLC consists of fifty-one members from the West Bank and thirty-seven from Gaza. Of these, some thirty members, or nearly 40 percent of all council members, are post-Oslo "returnees" to the West Bank and Gaza from PLO redoubts throughout the Arab world.[8] Twenty-six of these returnees are affiliated with Fatah, including longtime, high-ranking officials Nabil Amr, Rafiq al-Natshe, Ahmed Qurie (Abu Ala), and Abbas Zaki. In addition to being tied to the PLO, most elected members of the PLC have had a long history of "struggle." According to one source, seventy-eight of the eighty-eight council members were involved one way or another in Palestinian resistance against the Israeli occupation.[9]

Among the "non-returnees," or long-term residents of the West Bank and Gaza, elected members to the PLC also include a number of individuals from traditional, notable Palestinian families, including members of the Shaka'a (Nablus), Shawa (Gaza), and al-Masri (Nablus) clans. Another group strongly represented among West Bank and Gaza Palestinians are the younger generation of leaders of the *intifada* (uprising) who "cut their teeth" in Israeli prisons in the 1980s. This group includes such influential personalities as Marwan Barghouthi, Hussam Khader, and Hatim Abdul Qader.

As for the PLC's religious composition, the vast majority—eighty members, or 91 percent of the total membership—is Muslim. Seven of the remaining eight seats are allocated to Christians, and one seat—in the Nablus district—is allocated to a Samaritan.[10] Eighty-three PLC members are men; of the five women in the PLC, three hail from Gaza. Until the 1997 cabinet resignation of Minister of Education Hanan Ashrawi, two women—Intisar al-Wazir (Um Jihad), wife of former PLO official Khalil al-Wazir (Abu Jihad), being the other—held positions in Arafat's cabinet. As of December 1999, Minister of Social Affairs Um Jihad is the only female member of Arafat's thirty-three-member cabinet.

For the most part, council members are educated professionals in their early 50s. More than 85 percent of PLC members have attended college and received a bachelor's degree or higher. Thirteen members, or roughly 15 percent of the PLC's composition, have doctorates. The members of the council pursue a broad range of careers, from business to law, medicine, education, and many other professions. As compensation for their public service, members of the PLC are each paid approximately $30,000 per year.[11]

Standing Orders

Following the inauguration of the council on March 7, 1996, the first order of business was drafting the PLC's *al-Nitham al-Dakhli* (Standing Orders). These Standing Orders were adopted during the first regular council session, which convened March 21–22, 1996, and were subsequently amended in May 1997 and again in April 1998. The orders detail the operational regulations, organizational structure, and expected decorum on the floor of the PLC and provide details regarding the immunity of council members and procedures for Palestinian citizens to file petitions to, or complaints against, the council. Most important, however, the Standing Orders describe the legislative process.

According to the orders, the PLC is to sit for two four-month sessions per year, the first beginning in February and the second in September.[12] When the PLC is in session, meetings—called plenary sessions—are held every other week, usually on Tuesdays, Wednesdays, and Thursdays. Agendas are formalized and distributed to members prior to the meetings, and detailed minutes of the meetings are kept. Meetings are usually held in public, but they may if necessary—for security or other reasons—be held in secret or *in camera.* Standing Orders do not specifically designate activities for Sundays and Mondays, though generally these days are reserved for committee meetings.

The Standing Orders established twelve standing committees to "supervise and discuss the draft laws and proposals and issues that are referred by the Council or the Speaker." These committees and their chairs, as of January 2000, are listed in the table below.

Committee	Chairman
Budget and Financial Affairs	Azmi al-Shuyabi[1]
Council Affairs[2]	Ahmed Qurie (Abu Ala)
Economic	Jamal Shubaki
Education and Social Affairs	Abbas Zaki
Interior and Security	Fakhri Shaquora
Jerusalem	Ahmed Az-Zughayar
Land and Settlements	Salah Ta'mari
Legal	Abdul Karim Abu Salah
Natural Resources and Energy[3]	Ibrahim al-Habash
Parliamentary Monitoring	Hassan Kharesha
Political	Ziad Abu-Amr
Refugee[s] and Palestinians Abroad	Jamal al-Hindi

Notes:

[1] Shuyabi resigned in November 1999 and was replaced by Daoud al-Zeir, a legislator from Bethlehem. It was unclear at the time of publication whether Shuyabi would return.

[2] The Council Affairs Committee was actually established by PLC Resolution 3/4/264, April 16, 1998.

[3] The Natural Resources and Energy Committee has been disbanded. However, the Standing Orders have not been revised to reflect this change.

Office of the Council

Administrative affairs of the PLC are handled under the jurisdiction of the Office of the Council. This office, which consists of four primary officials including an elected Speaker, two deputy Speakers, and a secretary general, houses the highest profile officers in the PLC and directs the day-to-day matters of the legislature. The lion's share of the work in the Office of the Council falls upon the Speaker and the secretary general.

Perhaps for this reason, the office has subsequently become known as the "Office of the Speaker." In addition to the officials listed above, the office also maintains a significant administrative and professional staff currently headed by an office director and an administrative director.[13]

The Standing Orders of the PLC discuss in some detail the functions of the four elected officials serving in the Office of the Council. The duty of the Speaker is to "represent the Council and speak on its behalf and implement its will."[14] Likewise, it is the Speaker's role to determine the agenda, open, preside over, control, and close PLC meetings.[15] The Speaker's two elected deputies, who also serve in the Office of the Council, are tasked with assisting the Speaker in these responsibilities, as well as standing in for him when he is absent. Additionally, in accordance with *al-Qanun al-'Asasi* (the PLC Basic Law), which will be discussed below, the Speaker is in line to succeed the ra'is in the event of the latter's death.

The secretary general—the fourth elected official in the office—is tasked with running the secretariat, an organization trusted with the "legal, administrative, financial, media, foreign relations, public relations, and protocol affairs" of the PLC.[16] The secretariat is also responsible for implementing council decisions and keeping organizational records. The current officers serving in the Office of the Council were elected by a PLC vote in March 1999: Ahmed Qurie (Abu Ala), is the Speaker; Ibrahim Abu al-Naja is the first deputy; Ghazi Hanania, the second deputy; and Rawhi Fatouh, the secretary general.[17]

Legislative Process

The Palestinian legislative process is loosely based on the British parliamentary model. (See Appendix II.) Briefly stated, prior to its formal presentation, a draft law is vetted through a general discussion in the PLC. If the PLC then accepts the draft law, it is sent to the appropriate committees for amendments. After the draft law is amended, it is returned to the floor of the PLC for the first "reading," during which legislators discuss each article individually, put forth suggestions, and vote on each article. The draft law then returns to the committees for revision in conformity with the results of the discussion and vote, before being transferred back to the plenary for the second reading.

In one of the more interesting aspects of this legislative process, sometime after a law is initiated—but prior to its first reading—PLC members often participate in what are commonly known as *warshat 'amal* (workshops), something vaguely akin to "town hall meetings."[18] During these meetings, PLC members—usually members of a relevant committee—caucus with interested citizens and exchange views about a specific draft law. Typically, these workshops are organized by Palestinian nongovernmental organizations (NGOs) and are held throughout the West Bank and Gaza in auditoriums, conference rooms, or in particular NGO offices. Warshat 'amal provide an opportunity for average Palestinians to voice their concerns to legislators and provide input into pending legislation.

Depending on the issues under discussion, speakers may include PLC members or directors of prominent Palestinian NGOs, or both. The discussions are generally open to the public and are often punctuated by lively arguments, discussion, and debates among PLC members. During one such meeting in Gaza in the summer of 1998, for example, Gaza representative Jamila Sydam accused Minister of Industry Sa'adi al-Kurnz of making corrupt deals when he was chairman of the Budget Committee. Generally well attended, these workshops receive good coverage in the Palestinian press.

Not more than one month following the first reading, a draft law undergoes its second reading, during which proposed amendments are discussed and the draft law's individual articles are put to a final vote. At this point, if it is approved by an absolute majority, the draft law is considered "passed." But if the Council of Ministers (i.e., the executive authority cabinet) requests changes, the draft law must—even after receiving an absolute majority in the second reading—be submitted for a third reading. If the PLC ratifies the draft law after the second or third reading, it is forwarded within two weeks by the PLC Speaker to the ra'is for signature and publication in *al-Jarida al-Rasmiyya* (the *Official Gazette*), the journal in which all PA resolutions, edicts, executive appointments, corporate registrations, and laws are published. The ra'is has thirty days to either ratify the law or return it to the PLC with comments. *De jure*, there is no such thing as a "pocket veto," which the ra'is could use to kill a bill. In the event that the ra'is does not sign or return the draft law within thirty days, it should, according to the provisions of the Standing Orders, be published in the *Gazette* and become law.[19]

Should the ra'is formally veto or revise the text of a draft law, the legal procedure is less clear. Article 71 of the Standing Orders discusses this scenario, but the ambiguity of the language in this article is the subject of some controversy between the legislative and executive authorities. (This issue will be discussed in Chapter 3 in the context of the NGO law).

In addition to circumscribing the legislative process and internal administrative issues, the Standing Orders also outline the procedures by which members can question ministers, perform interrogatories, and hold votes of no confidence. These three procedures, which occur within the framework of the plenary session, constitute the PLC's most effective tools through which it can exercise power over the executive.

Supervision and Oversight

One of the PLC's primary responsibilities is the supervision and oversight of the executive authority—a crucial role that entails monitoring and reporting on the activities of the ra'is, the cabinet, the bureaucracy, and the security apparatus of the PA. Much of the PLC's legislative oversight of the executive is executed by the twelve standing committees, which carry out their own investigations and distribute reports based on their findings. When combined with the relatively free Palestinian press, legislative oversight can prove to be an extremely powerful tool to focus attention on PA indiscretions, mismanagement, and corruption—and to demand changes in the way the PA "does business."

Structurally, the PLC's oversight responsibilities reside in the *Lajnat al-Raqaba* (Supervision and Monitoring) Committee, one of the PLC's twelve standing committees. This committee has broad latitude in the areas it covers, but it focuses primarily on human rights abuses by PA security services, monopolies within the PA economy, financial irregularities within PA government agencies, corruption, and impediments to the free functioning of the judiciary. The Finance and Budget Committee—tasked with reviewing Ministry of Finance budgets and ensuring financial transparency in the executive—is also intimately involved in executive oversight.

In addition to the work of these committees, the PLC accomplishes its legislative oversight duties via its question period. Standing Order rules stipulate that the first thirty minutes of each legislative session are reserved for questions. During this period, legislators have the opportunity to pose direct and follow-up questions to ministers, security officials, and members of the PA executive authority. If a minister is scheduled to be questioned, attendance is theoretically mandatory.

Another tool of the legislature to exercise executive oversight is *istijwab* (interrogatories). According to the Standing Orders, interrogatories must be submitted in writing to the Speaker, who then determines an appropriate date—within ten days—for their presentation. According to this procedure, the member presents and explains the interrogatory before the council, and the minister then has the opportunity to reply. The nature of the questions directed toward the ministers during istijwab varies significantly—from overtly hostile to quasi-academic.

Exchanges during interrogatory sessions are frequently quite heated. In the event that a PLC member is not satisfied by an answer provided by an official, the legislator can refer the issue to an appropriate committee, call for further investigative hearings, or request a vote of no confidence in either a particular minister or the entire government. Since the PLC's inception, members have threatened to vote no confidence on many occasions. To date, however, the council has yet to withdraw confidence from the government or from a minister.

In addition to interrogatories, PLC committees can, in accordance with the bylaws, summon ministers and executive authority figures for hearings. As in the United States, PLC committee hearings are utilized to cover a broad and comprehensive range of subjects and, often, more than one minister or executive authority official is invited to attend a hearing to discuss a given subject. Although ministers are compelled to attend the hearings, the atmosphere is not necessarily (as is generally the case during interrogatories) acrimonious.

Miscellaneous Activities

In addition to its legislative and oversight roles, the PLC has also been involved with a number of smaller projects and issues of varying significance. These initiatives deserve mention, even if only to provide some perspective on the wide scope of PLC activities. On March 7, 1999, for example, the PLC sponsored its inaugural "Democracy Day," a celebration and commemoration of the PA's democratic achievements. Democracy Day initiated a week-long festival of sporting events and lectures on democracy for Palestinian youth.[20] One month later, in April 1999, the PLC organized a day dedicated to the study of books on democracy and legislatures.[21]

The PLC has also been consistent in its verbal support for women's issues. In March 1998, the PLC celebrated "Women's Day," marking the occasion by issuing a press release in which PLC Speaker Abu Ala recognized the role of Palestinian women in the struggle against Israel, and vowed to work to legislate equality for women in all fields.[22] PLC members have also been active in a campaign to raise the legal marriage age for Palestinian girls to 18 years old. In October 1998, PLC members Jamila Sydam, Kamal Ash Sharafi, and Abdel Karim Abu Saleh participated in a watershed discussion about the topic of early marriage.[23]

In addition to celebrations, campaigns, and legislation, the PLC devotes a great deal of time to discussing and debating more fundamental issues affecting the daily lives of Palestinians. In May 1998, for example, legislators discussed problems Palestinians were having at the Jordanian border checkpoint. This issue had come to the attention of some PLC members following reports that persons carrying Palestinian passports through the checkpoint were not being treated with the requisite respect. Legislators responded by agreeing to draft a letter to the Jordanian parliament.[24] PLC members have also spent time discussing procedures to curb the high level of Palestinian theft of automobiles from Israel. In June 1999, legislators tackled the important issue of revising and implementing commercial codes—an essential step to attract foreign investment to the PA.

Structurally, the PLC resembles a Western-style parliament. In terms of relative powers, though, a divergence has emerged between the *de jure* and *de facto* powers institutionally afforded the legislature in the PA political system. Oslo II appears to bestow the requisite powers to ensure a strong legislative authority, but the agreement's discussions of the legislative and executive are somewhat vague.

Much time is devoted to delineating the duties of the council in Oslo II, but a few clauses of the agreement also seem to totally undermine the council's authority by delegating sweeping powers to the executive authority. For example, Chapter 1, Article IX(2) extends the executive powers of the council—which are administered by the ra'is of the executive authority—to "all matters within its [the Palestinian Council's] jurisdiction . . . it shall include the power to formulate and conduct Palestinian policies and to supervise their implementation." Basically, this article provided an opportunity for Ra'is Arafat to supplant the PLC as the most powerful authority in the PA. Needless to say, this was not an opportunity the ra'is would miss.

Notes

1. The Palestinian Council was envisioned in the DOP and was fully defined in Oslo II. In addition to defining the legislature, Oslo II also defined the role of the executive and judicial authorities.

2. This number was determined by adding the number of pre-1967 West Bank representatives in the Jordanian parliament to the number of

representatives in the 1962 parliament in Gaza (set up by the Egyptians), and then adding a number of seats to reflect the increase in the Palestinian population since 1967. An additional six seats—bringing the total to eighty-eight members—were added later. Joel Singer, "The Emerging Palestinian Democracy under the West Bank and Gaza Strip Self-Governing Arrangements," *1997 Israel Yearbook on Human Rights* 26 (Zoetermeer, Netherlands: Martinus Nijhoff, 1997), pp. 313–365.

3. Israel Foreign Ministry, *Israeli–Palestinian Interim Agreement on the West Bank and Gaza Strip,* September 28, 1995, Chapter 1: The Council, Article IX(6), available from the Foreign Ministry Website, http://www.mfa.gov.il.

4. Ibid., Chapter 1: The Council, Article II(1).

5. After the signing of Oslo II, the Israelis agreed to a Palestinian request to add an additional six seats to the legislature, increasing its size from eighty-two to eighty-eight. Elections were held twenty-eight months after the signing of the Declaration of Principles and twenty months after the signing of the Gaza-Jericho Agreement.

6. The Gaza City district, for example, was allocated twelve seats in the council, including one seat specifically designated for a Christian. Faraj Bishara Saleem al-Saraf received more votes than any other Christian candidate but fewer votes than twenty-eight of the Muslim candidates in the district. Given the quota system, however, he was awarded the twelfth PLC seat for Gaza City.

7. According to the short biographies submitted by the council members and available on the PLC Website, http://www.pal-plc.org, four members consider themselves "close to Hamas," one member considers himself "Hamas," and one considers himself an "Islamist independent." Yet in spite of their declared affiliations, none of these members ran on a "Hamas" ticket. Muawya al-Masri, a legislator from Nablus, is representative of this phenomenon. Al-Masri ran as an "independent," but following his election, he described himself as "Hamas."

8. See members' biographies listed on the PLC Website.

9. *The Palestinian Council* (East Jerusalem: Jerusalem Media and Communication Centre [JMCC], Friedrich-Ebert-Stiftung, January 1998), Figure 5.

10. The Samaritan candidate, Saloum al-Kahin, received only 2,451 votes in the eight-seat Nablus district. Had he not been awarded the quota seat, al-Kahin would have finished forty-second in the race. Of the seven Christians in the PLC, only one—Hanan Ashrawi of Jerusalem,

who later served as minister of education—received enough votes to win a seat outright.

11. This amount is about fifteen times the local per capita gross national product. It would be roughly equivalent to U.S. senators making $450,000 per year.

12. In practice, the February session is usually delayed to coincide with March 7, the anniversary of the council's inauguration. March 7 is "Democracy Day" in the PA.

13. At the time of publication, these positions were held by Salah al-Ayan and Firas Yaghi, respectively.

14. See *al-Nitham al-Dakhli* [Standing Orders], Chapter 1, article 12.

15. Ibid.

16. Ibid., Chapter 1, article 11. "Foreign relations" is specified despite an explicit prohibition in Oslo II.

17. The vote for current members of the Office of the Council took place on March 7, 1999. Abu Ala received fifty-eight votes, while his opponent, Shaykh Suleiman Rumi, a legislator from Rafah, Gaza, received three votes. The other three incumbent candidates ran unopposed. The original officers elected in 1996 were Abu Ala, Rawhi Fatouh, Nahid al-Rayiss (first deputy), and Mitri Abu Aita (second deputy).

18. These workshops are also known as *halaqat niqash*, literally "discussion circles."

19. There are slightly different procedures for the passage of the Basic Law versus the passage of the budget law. These will be discussed later.

20. Democracy Day was established through PLC Resolution 3/19/363, January 10, 1999. Abu Ala's office was responsible for planning, supervising, and executing the campaign.

21. Na'el Musa, "al-Tashre'i yunathim yawman dirasiyyan hawl al-maktabat wa ilaqatuha bil-barlamanat" [The PLC Holds a Study Day about Libraries and their Relationships with Parliaments], *al-Hayat al-Jadida*, April 14, 1999, online in Arabic at http://www.alhayat-j.com.

22. "Bayan sahafi sader . . . yawm al-mar'a al-'alami" [A Press Release is Issued on International Women's Day], *al-Majlis al-Tashre'i Shahriyya Natiqa bi-ism al-Majlis al-Tashre'i al-Falastini* [Palestinian Legislative Council Monthly], no. 3 (March 1998), p. 44. There has been no indication of a significant and consistent increased focus on women's issues in the PLC since Women's Day 1998.

23. Nufood al-Bakri, "Mutalabah bi-raf'a al-ahliya al-qanuniyya lil-zawaj wa-taghir suluk al-mujtama'a tijah tatbiq al-qanun" [A Request to Raise the Marriage Age], *al-Hayat al-Jadida* online in Arabic, October 19, 1998.

24. See "al-Majlis al-Tashre'i al-Falastini: al-qararat" [The Decisions of the PLC], *al-Majlis al-Tashre'i Shahriyya*, no. 5 (1998), pp. 43–44.

Chapter 3

Imbalance in Governance: Executive Authority and the Oversight Role of the PLC

Israeli–Palestinian agreements specified a central role for the Palestinian Legislative Council (PLC) in Palestinian governance. Indeed, the PLC itself was originally designed to be the Palestinian Authority (PA), with the executive as only a subunit of the PLC. By the time the PLC was established in 1996, however, the PA had evolved into a three-branch system of government that, in form, roughly resembled the U.S. government. In contrast to the United States, however, no *de facto* system of checks and balances has prevailed in relations among the three "authorities." Although the PLC has a strong internal structure and efficient systems, the evolution of the PA has created an environment in which the legislature is ill-equipped to operate. In form, the PLC is both credible and functional; in practice, it is neither.

At least in part, the PLC has been disadvantaged by the existing legal framework of the PA, which is not particularly conducive to having an effective legislature. PA territory is governed by an amalgam of British mandatory law and Ottoman law, with Jordanian legal influences in the West Bank and Egyptian legal influences in Gaza. This mixture is complemented by Palestine Liberation Organization (PLO) laws from the Lebanon years.[1] Moreover, whereas the PLC derives its authority from Israeli–Palestinian agreements, the Oslo accords could not guarantee the PLC a significant role in Palestinian governance.

Thus, five years after the signing of the Israeli–Palestinian

Interim Agreement on the West Bank and the Gaza Strip (Oslo II), the PLC retains only a limited degree of influence in the Palestinian political landscape. Although the PA is equipped with the architecture of democratic institutions, the interactions among the three authorities do not resemble those of a democracy. The PLC, with its legislative and oversight agenda, is the sole governmental institution willing—sometimes—to act as a counterweight to the executive authority headed by the *ra'is* (president), Yasir Arafat. To date, however, the PLC has proven largely ineffective in carrying out its Oslo-mandated responsibilities. Because Arafat and his supporters so thoroughly dominate the executive authority—which controls all the financial and coercive resources of the PA and the PLO—it has proven difficult if not impossible for any group or organization to oppose him successfully on any given issue.

Relatively speaking, the executive is strong and all other Palestinian institutions are weak. The popularly elected Palestinian legislature is no exception. This simple fact has enabled the executive to ignore, undermine, and obstruct legislative will at every turn. To a certain extent, the PLC has endeavored to pursue its own mandated duties. Often, this has resulted in a direct confrontation with the executive authority. What has emerged since 1996 is a dynamic in which the legislature is engaged in a perpetual struggle to exert authority in the Palestinian political arena. Not surprisingly, the PLC has proven the loser in the vast majority of these clashes. These years of struggle have clearly taken a toll on the PLC. Although the PLC may have emerged as a stronger institution, both its membership and its stature in Palestinian politics have been diminished. As a result, many legislators have grown frustrated, disillusioned, and apathetic. Still others have been coopted by Arafat and the executive authority; when polled, Palestinians often say that their legislature is corrupt.[2]

What follows is a discussion of some of the factors that have contributed to the PLC's diminished condition. The organizational impotence of the PLC reflects the both the local political environment and the poor precedent set by the fledgling legislature. Briefly stated, the one-party system in the PA has produced a pronounced imbalance in Palestinian governance, which has only been exacerbated by PLC miscues. This chapter focuses on the composition of the elected membership of the PLC, the ongoing saga of *al-Qanun al-'Asasi* (the Basic Law), and the 1997 Corruption Report. The series of PLC missteps began with the Basic Law, which later evolved into a full-fledged institutional crisis.

The Basic Law

After the establishment of the PLC, the first items on the agenda for Palestinian lawmakers were the establishment of internal legal guidelines for the legislature and a legal framework for Palestinian society. In March 1996, the PLC passed its bylaws, *al-Nitham al-Dakhli* (the PLC Standing Orders). By that time, legislators were already working on the the Basic Law, which would later come to be known as the "Palestinian Constitution."

Basic Laws are staples of many Middle Eastern legal systems—including Saudi Arabia, Oman, and Israel. This fact was recognized in Oslo II, which encouraged the passage of a Palestinian basic law to govern the conduct of the Palestinian Interim Authority, provided that the law would "not be contrary to the provisions" of the Interim Agreement. As drafted, the Palestinian Basic Law covers a broad range of issues, including the protection of civil liberties and personal freedoms, as well as the separation of legislative, executive, and judicial powers.

Substance of the Law

Structurally, the Basic Law is divided into eight sections. The introduction provides an overview of the entire law. Chapter 1 establishes the principle of separation of powers among the legislative, executive, and judicial authorities; declares Jerusalem the capital of Palestine; and establishes *shari'a* (Islamic law) as "a main source" of all Palestinian legislation. Chapter 2 sets guidelines for human rights in the PA and includes clauses banning torture, arbitrary arrest, and illegal search and seizure, as well as clauses assuring freedom of religion, expression, association, and the press. Chapter 3 is a summary of the legislative procedures detailed in the PLC Standing Orders.

Chapter 4 of the Basic Law discusses the structure of the executive authority—which consists of the office of the ra'is and the cabinet ministries. This chapter addresses the responsibilities and powers of the ra'is vis-à-vis the PLC and limits the term of office of the ra'is to the end of the five-year transitional, or interim, period following the signing of the Oslo Declaration of Principles (this period technically ended May 4, 1999).[3] Additionally, it appoints the ra'is commander-in-chief of *al-qa'id al-'ala lil-quwat al-falastiniyya* (the Palestinian [armed] forces). Most important, however, Chapter 4 focuses on the mechanisms of accountability for the executive, including ministers and ministries and requiring, among other things, full financial disclosure from cabinet ministers before they take office. Likewise, this chapter mandates the establishment of an office to monitor and provide oversight of the executive's administrative and financial apparatuses.

Chapter 5 provides a brief overview of the role, structure, and procedures of the judicial authority, and it reviews some of the fundamental principles of jurisprudence in the PA.[4] Judicial independence is defined as a *sine qua non* of the system, with systemic transparency—such as public hearings—mandated as an essential judiciary practice. The chapter also authorizes implementation of the death penalty, given the prior approval of the ra'is. Notably, Chapter 5 places personal status issues—such as marriage and divorce—under the jurisdiction of shari'a courts.

Emergency situations—including war, invasion, armed insurrection, and natural disasters—are among the topics addressed in Chapter 6. According to the provisions of this chapter, emergency situations declared by the ra'is can last for only thirty days unless otherwise extended by a two-thirds majority of the PLC. In situations such as these, the law dictates that authorized courts must review all detentions within fifteen days and that all detainees have the right to a lawyer.

The final section, Chapter 7, discusses the Basic Law itself, which is recognized as the Palestinian "constitution." As such, the law requires a two-thirds majority vote in the PLC for any amendment. It also stipulates that the Basic Law will exist until a new basic law or a constitution is passed.

Legislative History

The legislative history of the Basic Law typifies the experience of the PLC, and particularly the dynamic between the legislative and executive authorities. In April 1996, Palestinian legislators resolved to draft a "temporary constitution."[5] One month later, the PLC resolved to begin discussion of the draft constitution—which would later be known as the Basic Law.[6] An initial copy of the draft law appeared in the Palestinian daily *al-Ayyam* on June 16, 1996. Discussions on the Basic Law continued in the legislature through September 1, when the PLC passed the Basic Law on its first reading, and referred it to the cabinet of ministries for comment.[7]

The Basic Law was not discussed on the floor of the PLC again until July 1997—some thirty-eight sessions later.[8] Despite an eleven-month interval, the executive had neglected to submit any comments or critique on the law's first reading. Nonetheless, the PLC proceeded to discuss revisions for the second reading. The legislators made some minor changes and additions during the second reading, and after several sessions of discussions and deliberations, on September 17, 1997, they passed the Basic Law on its second reading.

As with the first reading, the executive authority did not comment on the second reading of the draft law. The PLC therefore decided to provide the executive with one more opportunity by initiating a third reading. On October 2, 1997, the PLC passed the Basic Law on its third reading and submitted it to Arafat for critique or ratification. But once again, Arafat neither signed the law nor returned it to the legislature with comments, nor did he authorize its publication in *al-Jarida al-Rasmiyya* (the *Official Gazette*). In effect, Arafat ignored the Basic Law.

Basic Law Ignored

In the aftermath of this affront to legislative authority, PLC member and elder statesman Haidar Abdel Shafi resigned from the legislature. Although Abdel Shafi admitted that he had been considering tendering his resignation for some time because of PA corruption, it appears that the primary reason for his resignation was the complete disregard for the legislature exhibited by Arafat's executive authority.[9] When asked about his resignation, Abdel Shafi said, with sadness, "The council is not functioning. It's being paralyzed, . . . marginalized. There is no reason for me to stay. There's nothing to do."[10] After his departure from the PLC, Abdel Shafi formed a new political party called the Democratic Construction Movement (*Harakat al-Bina' al-Democrati*). He remains a vocal and popular critic of Arafat and the PA executive.[11]

Two years after the PLC passed it, Arafat has still not signed the Basic Law. Several explanations have been suggested for why he has refused to do so. Accountability and balance of power among the judicial, legislative, and executive authorities are the fundamental underpinnings of the Basic Law. It seems likely that Arafat's resistance to the law represents his opposition to limitations on his own executive authority. Arafat, critics say, would never sign a law that would diminish his power. PLC Political Committee chair Ziad Abu-Amr articulated this perspective when he attributed executive disrespect for the PLC to "the political culture of the executive authority [i.e., Arafat], which refuses to accept the principle of accountability as a basis of relations between the executive and the PLC."[12] Other legislators have not been as kind in their assessments. In December 1998, PLC member Hussam Khader, frustrated by Arafat's obduracy and refusal to accept legislative oversight or any limitations on executive power, proposed in disgust that the PLC declare Arafat "god of Palestine."[13]

In contrast to the explanations focusing on Arafat's authoritarian tendencies, some rationalize his behavior by explaining it in terms of the highly politicized environment in which he operates. It is rumored, for example, that Arafat agonized over the Basic Law—that he feared its ratification would induce a split in the PLO because it dealt with so many controversial issues of concern to Palestinians residing both inside and outside of the PA. Many Palestinians, especially the beneficiaries of PA largess, maintain that the Basic Law—and particularly Chapter 1, which deals with the issue of Jerusalem and the status of Palestinians—was the primary source of disagreement between Arafat and the PLC.[14] Such a major decision, some Palestinian officials say, would require Palestinian National Council (PNC) approval. Other Palestinians, like Haidar Abdel Shafi, dismiss this rationale:

> Arafat adopted an obstructive attitude, saying that the [PLC] is not entitled to deal with this issue, that the Basic Law fell within the domain of the Palestine National Council. This was not logical. Conceding that the PNC is the highest organ in the PLO, it really has nothing to do with the interim period.[15]

A few additional explanations that strain credulity have also gained currency. For example, PA minister of social affairs Intisar al-Wazir (Um Jihad) maintains that Israel opposed the Basic Law and interfered with—and ultimately prevented—its ratification because it considered the law to be in contravention of the Oslo accords.[16] Others believe that Washington encouraged Arafat's opposition to the Basic Law because it contained provocative clauses—like the "declaration of Jerusalem as the capital of Palestine"—which are contrary to the PLC's mandate in Oslo II. But some ascribe an even more nefarious intent to Washington, suggesting that a U.S. preference for Arafat's authoritarian but stable government prevailed over the competing claims of Palestinian democrats who were the proponents of the Basic Law.

Rumors, allegations, and conspiracy theories aside, the fact is that the United States did officially support the passage of the Basic Law and even lobbied Arafat for its ratification. Edward Abington, consul general in Jerusalem from 1993 to 1996, met with Arafat a number of times and encouraged him to ratify the law. In February 1997, articulating U.S. policy at the time, he stated, "the draft [of the Basic Law] has been languishing on Chairman Arafat's desk for far too long. It needs to be enacted so that the Council can get on with its business."[17] This position was clearly consistent with Washington's stated policy of encouraging democracy in the region. Insofar as the "Jerusalem" clause of the Basic Law prejudiced the "final status" agreements between the sides, Washington did consider the clause to be "unhelpful," but at the end of the day, U.S. policymakers were convinced that the law would be more helpful than harmful.[18] In any case, although the U.S. consul general in Jerusalem made some effort to encourage the Basic Law, Washington was not a strong and forceful public advocate for its ratification.

Both the Basic Law and the PLC Standing Orders—neither of which have been ratified by Arafat—should, according to the procedures mandated by the PLC, be recognized as law in the PA. Indeed, the Oslo accords provide the basis for these legal measures. Even so, Arafat has refused to accept the laws as legally binding.

The root of the problem, at least procedurally, lies with the *Official Gazette*, the legal registry of the PA. PLC Standing Orders stipulate that, after thirty days without comment from the executive, a draft law published in the *Official Gazette* becomes law. This stipulation, however, represents a dilemma for the PLC. The *Official Gazette* is published by the Ministry of Justice—part of the executive authority controlled by Arafat—and nothing appears in the publication without Arafat's permission. To date, Arafat has prohibited publication of both the Basic Law and the Standing Orders in the *Gazette*. Until the laws are ratified or are published in the *Gazette*—or both—Arafat's obligation to adhere to the prescriptions therein remains unclear from a legal perspective.

Many PLC members have grown exceedingly frustrated with Arafat's ability—and predilection—to ignore legislative will. This situation—in which PLC members lack the ability to have passed legislation recognized as law—has come to resemble a Catch-22. The PLC has established procedures to override Arafat, but Arafat refuses to ratify these procedures.

In 1997, after it became apparent that the publication of laws would become another in a litany of difficulties for the PLC, the Legal Committee chairman suggested to his colleagues that the legislature should circumvent Arafat and the *Official Gazette* altogether by voting to instead publish PLC legislation in the PLC's own journal, *al-Majlis al-Tashre'i Shahriyya Natiqa bi-ism al-Majlis al-Tashre'i al-Falastini* (Palestinian Legislative Council Monthly). Unfortunately, according to the chairman, this initiative was strongly opposed and ultimately stymied by the overwhelming majority of pro-Arafat members in the legislature.[19]

A One-Party System Emerges

Even from the establishment of the PLC, it seemed that the deck was stacked in Arafat's favor. First, thirty-four of the eighty-eight elected PLC members were, at the time of their elections, either PA officials, Fatah officials, or in other positions closely affiliated with the PA government apparatus. Likewise, many of the "independent" candidates who were elected to the PLC were in fact, supporters or members of Fatah who had not received the party nomination for their districts, but who stood for election anyway. Additionally, other non-PLO parties that did run for election—such as the National Movement for Change and Haidar Abdel Shafi's party at the time, the NDC—were neither well organized nor well funded. Perhaps most important, though, is the fact that the Islamists—the only alternative parties or political entities to Fatah with real organizational structures and strong popular support—boycotted the elections.

These factors contributed to a situation in which some two-thirds to three-fourths of the eighty-eight elected members of the PLC were Fatah or Fatah sympathizers. In addition to lending some credibility to the notion that the PLC is "corrupt," the close affiliation of many PLC members with Fatah and the PLO—even those members elected as self-declared "independents"—has also contributed to a widespread perception that the PLC is a rubber stamp for Arafat's executive branch.[20]

Overall, the composition of the PLC is not one that promotes good governance. A rough assessment could arguably characterize the legislature's membership as follows: Fifteen to twenty members are active, deeply committed to democratic processes, and devoted to establishing the legislature as a legitimate counterbalance to the executive authority; twenty-five to thirty—primarily ministers—are beneficiaries of Arafat's largess, have been coopted by the executive authority, and are unwilling to act against executive will; ten to twelve are close to the executive and are unlikely to act as an opposition; and twenty-five others do not take an active role in legislative proceedings.[21]

The effect of Arafat's pressure on the composition of the PLC—and its predisposition to oppose him—has been remarkable. One particularly striking example is the case of Rafiq al-Natshe, a widely respected legislator from Hebron. Al-Natshe, a long time PLO functionary and Fatah stalwart, was, until recently, well known for being a vociferous critic of Arafat and the Oslo process. He served on the legal and political committees of the legislature in the PLC's second year until, during a cabinet shakeup, Arafat offered—and al-Natshe accepted—the position of PA minister of labor. During a recent discussion with al-Natshe, although the minister was still critical of Arafat's human rights record, it was clear that he had become, surprisingly, a supporter of Oslo.[22]

To be fair, the situation in the PA resembles something akin to a presidential–parliamentary system in which strict party discipline is expected and demanded. It is therefore not particularly surprising that, with such an overwhelming majority, the chief executive would be able to run roughshod over the parliament. Arafat, however, goes well beyond the standard principles of party discipline. He ignores the legislature, knowing that his power of personality, high degree of popular support, and the institutional confusion that prevails in the PA will enable him to carry the day. In the end, the PLC typically goes along with him. Perhaps in large part out of fear of the unknown—that is, of who might replace Arafat—the PLC is, in a way, compelled to defer to the ra'is.

Office of the Council

Perhaps more problematic than the composition of the council and the dwindling number of legislators willing to oppose executive dictate is the leadership of the PLC itself. This leadership is housed in the Office of the Council and runs the PLC secretariat, the organization charged with handling the legal, administrative, and financial matters of the legislature. Despite what appears to be a well-organized structure, the Office of the Council has proven to be—with the exception of Arafat—the legislature's own worst enemy.

To be sure, the Office of the Council has encountered significant difficulties related to legislative and administrative development in its first three years. A main obstacle in the administrative development of the PLC has been the secretariat, which is run by Secretary General Rawhi Fatouh. In addition to his position in the Office of the Council, Fatouh simultaneously serves as a PLC member from Rafah and is a high-ranking Fatah party official in Gaza. With all of these responsibilities, according to one observer, Fatouh has been able to devote only part of his time to administrative issues in the PLC—a full-time position in and of itself. As a result, administrative development in the PLC has suffered.

Recognizing this problem, in January 1999 the Office of the Council appointed Mahmoud Labadi, then-head of studies and publications at the Palestinian Economic Council for Development and Reconstruction (PECDAR), as full-time administrative manager of the PLC, with the title of director general of the council.[23] Some of his priorities have included ensuring transparent hiring processes in the legislature, implementing standardized operating procedures, holding weekly staff meetings, and improving inter-departmental communications among the nearly three hundred PLC employees.

Although hiring a full-time administrator to run the PLC secretariat was a necessary and positive step, the choice of Labadi—another long-time PLO functionary—has been problematic. Labadi himself has emerged as an Arafat "company man" who does not advocate a robust, independent legislature. In fact, Labadi maintains that the crisis nature of the

Palestinian political climate necessitates a PLC subservient to executive will.[24] For example, when asked about an incident in August 1999 during which Arafat ignored the legislature's will and unilaterally ratified his own version of a law on Palestinian nongovernmental organizations (NGOs), Labadi unapologetically endorsed Arafat's behavior as an appropriate executive prerogative.[25] "This is fine," he said, "the president has the right."[26]

In the end, the Labadi appointment may retard the development of the legislature, but it is essentially an administrative position that has only a minor effect on the overall disposition of the legislature in Palestinian governance. As far as influence is concerned, the most important position in the legislature is that of PLC Speaker. Ahmed Qurie (Abu Ala), a longtime, high-ranking PLO bureaucrat and architect of the Oslo accords, has served as Speaker since the PLC's establishment in 1996. To the world, Abu Ala is the "face" of the PLC; he meets with foreign delegations and heads of foreign parliaments, serves as a traveling goodwill ambassador, and represents "Palestinian democracy" abroad. In 1998, Abu Ala led a PLC delegation to the U.S. Congress and met with then–Speaker of the House Newt Gingrich; in 1999, he made a high-profile visit to Israel's Knesset, meeting with Israeli Speaker Avraham Burg.

By and large, legislators commend the intentions and service of Abu Ala. He is, according to one former diplomat, a supporter of democracy who has been genuinely frustrated by Arafat's obstructionist behavior toward the PLC. At the same time, however, Abu Ala's tenure as Speaker has proven problematic in the development of the legislature as a counterbalance to the executive. The problem does not lie with Abu Ala *per se*, but rather with the Palestinian political landscape and the transformation of the PLO from a government in exile to an interim governing authority of a future state.

The stress of transition is clearly reflected in the conflicts faced by Abu Ala in the council's initial years. Prior to his election as Speaker, Abu Ala had spent his entire professional career as a high-ranking PLO functionary, a position that placed a premium on both party loyalty and personal loyalty to Arafat. As a Speaker operating within a "presidential system" of government, however, Abu Ala has been propelled into what is necessarily a structurally adversarial position to Arafat. But contrary to the demands of his position, the Speaker has not been a forceful advocate on behalf of the council vis-à-vis the executive.[27] Abu Ala stands somewhere on the continuum between the executive and legislative branches.

The inherent tension between Abu Ala's political career and his position within a one-party system of government has been detrimental to the development of the PLC. In short, PLC leadership in the Office of the Council has not taken steps to create and promote an effective system of checks and balances in the PA. The most visible and damaging consequence of this conduct is that the PLC has rarely opposed executive will.

How has this tension been reflected? According to accounts, Abu Ala has been tireless in his efforts to mediate and decrease the hostility between the executive and legislative authorities. Although most legislators are sympathetic to efforts to maintain "national unity," some believe that Abu Ala's conciliation efforts have undercut the authority of the PLC. He has, for example, consistently dissuaded legislators from placing votes of no confidence and other forms of executive censure on PLC meeting agendas.[28] In effect, by ignoring the will of the council in this regard, Abu Ala violates PLC Standing Orders. By refusing to exercise one of the legislature's only tools of coercion against the executive, Abu Ala has weakened rather than strengthened the PLC.

In essence, according to the Standing Orders, the Speaker's role is merely to facilitate PLC proceedings, but given the tenuous relationship between the legislative and executive authorities, executing the Speaker's duties has been particularly difficult. To manage this relationship and maintain consensus in the PLC, Abu Ala has transformed the position of Speaker into more of a "leadership" role. This fundamental shift—from "facilitator" to "leader"—may have played some part in preventing the PLC from developing into an effective legislative body. What happens during PLC floor discussions is illustrative of this subtle distinction. Article 12 of the Standing Orders specifies that the Speaker may participate in the discussions, provided the Speaker "vacate the chair while doing so." In violation of the orders, however, Abu Ala rarely if ever steps down from the Speaker's chair to participate in debates. This example may seem trivial, but it is indicative of how the Speaker perceives his role.

Critics of Abu Ala also point out that he has sided with the executive against the legislature on several issues that many consider to be "support for democracy" litmus tests. The issue of local elections is one such example. In April 1998, PLC members questioned Minister of Local Government Sa'eb Erekat as to why he had opposed local elections in Tulkarm in favor of the continued executive appointment of members of the local council. At the end of the question period, Abu Ala stated that he, like Erekat, supported elections at the earliest possible opportunity. Abu Ala then referred the issue to the PLC Security and Interior Committee.[29] Not surprisingly, this committee—like the executive authority—has supported an indefinite delay of local elections.[30] By referring the issue to the committee, Abu Ala effectively sided with the executive position opposing local elections.

On another occasion, Abu Ala prohibited two U.S. Agency for International Development (USAID) technical assistance initiatives intended to improve the oversight capacity of the PLC.[31] In 1998 and early 1999, Associates for Rural Development (ARD), the lead U.S. government contractor working with the PLC, had successfully implemented a small pilot project designed to teach PLC members and staff how to execute public "hearings." The topic of the test-case hearing was the regulation and distribution of pharmaceuticals in the PA. In 1999, two PLC members requested similar assistance from ARD to hold public hearings about the Fiscal Year (FY) 1999 PA budget and the status of human rights. According to PLC legislator and Human Rights Committee member Abdel Jawad Saleh, shortly after planning was underway, a request from Abu Ala to ARD quickly put an end to this endeavor.[32]

More recently, in the spring of 1999, it was alleged that Abu Ala pressured the PLC Budget Committee to accelerate the budget review process. In May 1999, after the budget morass took a turn for the worse, PLC insiders whispered that Abu Ala issued a "gag order," essentially forbidding Azmi Shuyabi, chairman of the Budget Committee, from holding a press conference to discuss the budget. When Shuyabi resigned as Budget Committee chairman in November 1999, he excoriated Abu Ala for refusing to allow the PLC to proceed with a vote of no confidence in the PA minister of finance.[33]

Abu Ala's position on local elections, his alleged "gagging" of Azmi Shuyabi, and his refusal to allow no-confidence votes to be placed on the PLC agenda are indicative of a larger problem within the Office of the Speaker and the PLC in general—that is, the domination of the ra'is and his success at coopting the leaders of the PLC and a plurality of its members.

Supervision and Oversight

Supervision and oversight constitute another area in which the PLC has *de jure* but not *de facto* powers. Because the ra'is often chooses not to ratify laws that the legislature has passed, many Palestinian legislators maintain that oversight of the executive is an even more important duty than legislating. Kamal Ash Sharafi, a Palestinian legislator from Jabaliyya, Gaza, is the former head of the PLC Monitoring Committee, tasked with monitoring the executive. Ash Sharafi maintains that the system of legislative monitoring is functioning properly, but it has been hampered by the fact that the executive disregards PLC decisions. "There are results," he says, "but no judiciary to implement them."[34]

Since the establishment of the legislature, the Monitoring Committee has issued reports about monopolies, Israeli human rights violations, and political prisoners in the PA. Indeed, the Monitoring Committee report on political prisoners became a locus of controversy when it was released in January 1999. The report discussed the predicament of the nearly three hundred Islamist "political prisoners" in PA jails, many of whom had been imprisoned without charge by the PA since 1996. In addition to demanding the prisoners' release, the committee's report was critical of the PA security services, which had previously refused to release the prisoners despite judicial directives to do so. More recently, in November 1999, a report was issued alleging that branches of the PA security forces, including the General Security Service and the Protective Security Service as well as Military Intelligence, were engaged in the systematic practice of extorting money from Palestinian businessmen.[35]

The Corruption Report

Of the documents issued by the Monitoring Committee, the publication that put the committee on the map was the *Special Committee Report Concerning the Annual Report of the General Comptroller Office for 1996*, better known as the "Corruption Report."[36] Four members of the Monitoring Committee participated in the nine-member Special Committee that authored the report.[37] Issued in June 1997, the report presented a highly detailed portrait of executive authority graft, nepotism, and mismanagement that allegedly resulted in the disappearance of more than $300 million from PA coffers. It also fingered several PA ministers as leading culprits in the corruption, including Minister of Planning and International Cooperation Nabil Sha'ath, Minister of Culture Yasser Abed Rabbo (who currently serves as information minister), Civil Affairs Minister Jamil Tarifi, and Minister of Transportation Ali Qawasmeh.

The accusations leveled against the ministers ranged from the relatively minor to the outrageous. For example, the committee found that the Ministry of Culture had paid 26,851 shekels (or roughly $7,000) for the installation of central heating in the rented home of Abed Rabbo. Chapter 17 of the report described the diversion of an unspecified amount of public funds in the Ministry of Planning and International Cooperation for personal use by Minister Sha'ath. Of all the charges, however, the allegations against the Ministry of Civil Affairs proved the most defamatory. In addition to citing the apparently standard practice in this ministry of granting customs exemptions on luxury automobiles to high-ranking security officials and relatives, the report also described a complicated system whereby Minister Tarifi received substantial kickbacks for his ministry's role in protecting a cement monopoly in the West Bank.[38]

The Corruption Report was big news, covered by the domestic and international press. PLC members publicly clamored for the resignations of those accused. When hearings were held in the PLC, the three aforementioned ministers were provided with the opportunity to defend themselves against the allegations, but a PLC general session vote following the ministers' testimonies failed to exonerate any of them. In fact, the general session confirmed the Corruption Report, which was then delivered to Arafat. At that point, it was assumed by many that the indicted ministers would be fired. Instead of dismissing the ministers charged with corruption, however, Arafat ignored the recommendations of the PLC and reconstituted his cabinet—enlarging it by an additional eight ministers, and firing none.[39] In a subsequent vote, a majority of PLC members voted confidence in Arafat's reconstituted cabinet, which included the three ministers originally charged with corruption.

Pattern of Disrespect

The Corruption Report—and the subsequent executive inaction—is indicative of the lack of respect accorded the PLC as an institution. Like other forms of "opposition" in the PA, the PLC is viewed by the executive as a threat to be controlled, coopted, or destroyed. Executive abuse of legislative authority is not just limited to occasional slights. It has become a pattern of behavior that prevents the PLC from performing nearly all of its mandated tasks, particularly in terms of its oversight role. As the Corruption Report illustrated, the executive ignores the findings of significant PLC oversight procedures and regularly impedes progress in oversight proceedings.

Many ministers and PA security officials, for example, routinely disregard PLC committee requests and refuse to appear for questioning, hearings, and other parliamentary inquiries. The instance of Musa Arafat, chief of Military Intelligence (and nephew of the ra'is), is particularly instructive. When asked in December 1998 to appear before the PLC, he refused, stating, "The man in charge of the security services is the head of the PA, and we will not say anything except to our leadership. I will not go to the Legislative Council to testify, and I am not willing to deal with them."[40]

Although no accurate records are available detailing the percentage of executive authority officials who refuse to attend, participate, and fully cooperate in mandatory PLC oversight activities, the practice is rampant. High-profile no-shows in 1999 included Minister of Justice Freih Abu Meddien, who declined to attend a formal session of the PLC on January 7, 1999, to answer questions about prisoner release and due process, and Minister of Finance Muhammad Nashashibi, who since 1996 has repeatedly refused to appear before the legislature to answer inquiries about late budgets. The frequency of refusals has taken a toll on the PLC's willingness to demand attendance. Each year from 1996 through 1998, members increased the number of requests for attendance, but in 1999, the number of PLC requests dropped precipitously.[41]

In addition to the ongoing executive affronts to the PLC's legislative enterprises, there have also been occasions in which the executive authority violates the physical integrity of PLC members. Although the Basic Law establishes that all legislative council members are immune from questioning, prosecution, search, or any other type of harassment,[42] there have been cases in which legislators have been threatened or placed in harm's way. In one such episode, PLC member Hatim Abdul Qader was hospitalized for two days after he was severely beaten by PA security forces in the West Bank town of al-Bireh. Abdul Qader was one of thirty-one Palestinian legislators who had gathered outside the house of the Awadallah family in protest on August 25, 1998. (The family had been placed under house arrest following the escape from prison of Hamas bomb-maker Imad Awadallah two weeks earlier.) During a scuffle that occurred when the legislators attempted to enter the house, members of the PA Preventative Security Forces (PSF) manhandled several legislators. On August 26, the PLC convened in special session in Ramallah and passed a resolution calling for the immediate suspension—pending the results of an investigation—of Jibril Rajoub, head of the PSF in the West Bank.

In response to the PLC's outcry, Arafat established a committee on August 27 to investigate the incident. Essentially, by establishing this committee, Arafat buried the issue. While in the hospital, Abdul Qader received a telephone call from Arafat, who suggested that he "not make a big deal" out of the incident.[43] No punitive measures were taken against Rajoub or the PSF.

At other times, if not beaten, legislators have been threatened or harassed by the security forces. In 1996, PA security forces prevented PLC members from meeting with citizens of Nablus to discuss PA human rights violations. At the time, PLC member Haidar Abdel Shafi described the harassment as a blatant "violation of the[ir] immunity" as legislators.[44] Moreover, in 1998, PLC member Hassan Kharesha was informed by security officials that certain legislators might be physically harmed "after their terms and [legislative] immunity expire."[45]

Some of the most blatant and in fact unprecedented cases of violation of parliamentary immunity occurred in December 1999 as this study was going to press. In November 1999, twenty Palestinians—including two former mayors, nine academics, and nine members of the PLC—signed and distributed a leaflet implicating Arafat in the rampant corruption of the PA.[46] In the aftermath of the leaflet's distribution, several of the academics were arrested, and there was discussion that the immunity of the parliamentary signatories would be revoked. One Islamist legislator from Nablus, Mu'awweh al-Masri, refused to recant his remarks. On December 1, al-Masri was shot in the foot by a group of masked men in broad daylight while he walking down the street. Although there is no conclusive evidence of official executive authority involvement in the shooting, al-Masri appeared convinced that the PA was behind this attempt at physical intimidation.[47] The incident has its precedents. In August 1995, Abdul Sattar Qassem, a professor at al-Najah University, was shot in the leg while walking in Nablus; he had not long beforehand made some remarks critical of Arafat. Perhaps not coincidentally, Qassem was also a signatory to this 1999 leaflet.

The parliamentary immunity of another signatory to this pamphlet—Abdul Jawad Salah, a 70-year-old legislator from Ramallah and former mayor of al-Bireh—was also violated in December 1999. On December 16, Salah was severely beaten by seven members of the Palestinian Security Forces while participating in a demonstration outside the General Intelligence Detention Center in Jericho. The demonstrators were protesting the continued detention, without charge or trial, of three of the signatories to the petition.

If the most recent incidents of gratuitous violations of parliamentary immunity are any indication, the practice is becoming more routine. Not surprisingly, the pattern of disrespect exhibited by the executive toward the PLC—both in terms of physical abuse and the abuse of power used to curtail legislative and oversight prerogatives—has had an extremely damaging effect on the legislature. When the PLC was established, members were confident of their ability to effect change in Palestinian society. Four years later, many legislators are understandably demoralized.

What occurred en route to the passage of the Basic Law and following the publication of the Corruption Report is indicative of the consequences that executive behavior has had on PLC initiatives. When the PLC ratified Arafat's enlarged cabinet in the aftermath of the Corruption Report, in effect, it sanctioned executive authority corruption and compromised its own credibility on issues of governmental transparency. Since this episode, the PLC has not been as ambitious in its oversight endeavors.

The response of the PLC after the publication of the petition (which resulted in the two aforementioned violations of parliamentary immunity) was also quite telling. PLC members did not condemn Arafat for corruption, or even request an investigation into the allegations of the petition signed by their colleagues. Rather, the PLC convened in special session in Gaza to condemn the legislators who criticized Arafat.

At one time, it had been hoped that the PLC would serve as a counterbalance to the executive authority. As the imbalance in the legislative–executive relationship grows more pronounced, however, the chances for an effective and activist PLC decline. This trend shows no sign of reversing. (See Appendix III.)

Notes

1. One example, among many, is an obscure PLO law called the "Palestinian Penal Code of 1979," which is still used with regularity in the PA.

2. For example, 51 percent of Palestinians believe that corruption exists in the PLC; see Center for Palestine Research and Studies (CPRS), *Palestinian Public Opinion Poll no. 42,* July 15–17, 1999.

3. Article 57 of the Basic Law states that the president shall promulgate the laws after their approval from the PLC within thirty days from the date on which he is informed about them. The president can return the laws to the council within the same period accompanied by his comments and reasons for objection. Otherwise, the laws shall be considered promulgated and shall be published immediately in the *Official Gazette.* As for the interim period, it is still unclear whether the term of the ra'is and the PLC will be extended through the end of the negotiations with the Israelis. According to Clause 53, after the transition period is over, new elections must be held for the ra'is. In February 1999, Osama Abu Saffiya, director general of the Elections Committee, declared that the term of the PLC (and presumably the ra'is) could be extended indefinitely by Arafat's decree.

4. The judiciary law was passed by the PLC in December 1998, but it has not been ratified, published in the *Official Gazette,* or implemented by the executive.

5. PLC Resolution 1/3/8, passed April 3–4, 1996.

6. The council resolved to call the law the "Basic Law" during the twelfth PLC session, in Ramallah, which convened July 10–11, 1996. See The Basic Law (*al-Qanun al-'Asasi*), which appears in both English and Arabic on the PLC website, at http://www.pal-plc.org.

7. PLC Resolution 1/9/91, resolved session 19, passed August 28–29, 1996.

8. Palestinian Center for Human Rights, *al-Majlis al-Tashre'i al-Falastini* [The Palestinian Legislative Council] (Gaza City: al-Markaz al-Falastini li-huquq al-'Insan [Palestinian Center for Human Rights (PCHR)], November 1998), p. 45.

9. See Ahmad Bukhari, "Abd-al-Shafi Explains Reasons for Resignation," *Jerusalem Times*, October 10, 1997.

10. Steve Rodan, "Abdul Shafi refuses to retract resignation," *Jerusalem Post*, October 17, 1997.

11. In Abdel Shafi's absence, the PLC has had only eighty-seven members for the past year and a half. After Abdel Shafi resigned, the mechanism was started for a special election in Gaza City to fill the empty seat, but a decision from the PA high court (involving an interpretation of the Election Law) canceled the elections. The Gaza City constituency therefore remains underrepresented in the PLC by one seat.

12. PCHR, *al-Majlis al-Tashre'i al-Falastini*, p. 50.

13. Deborah Sontag, "There's No Bossing a Democracy, Arafat Learns," *New York Times*, December 13, 1998, p. 1.

14. PCHR, *al-Majlis al-Tashre'i al-Falastini*, p. 49.

15. Interview of Haider Abdel Shafi, *Middle East Policy* 6, no. 1 (June 1998), pp. 109–115.

16. Author interview with Intisar al-Wazir, February 18, 1999. Whereas al-Wazir was generally supportive of Arafat's position, she likewise maintained that Palestinians from outside the PA would have to be given the opportunity to vote on the Basic Law as well.

17. U.S. Consul General Edward Abington's remarks during a USAID–PLC grant ceremony in Gaza, February 4, 1997. Online at http://www.usis-israel.org.il.

18. Interestingly, in contrast to Abington's comments on the matter, the State Department Press Office is unambiguous in stating that the Basic Law is an internal affair of the Palestinians, and that the United States takes no official position.

19. Author interview with Abdel Karim Abu Saleh, chair, PLC Legal Committee, February 17, 1999.

20. The PLC is not exactly a "rubber stamp"; indeed, there exists a small, core group of dedicated, apparently independent-minded members

who are not afraid to oppose executive decisions. In polls, roughly one-third of Palestinians describe their own PLC district representative as "good" or "very good." See CPRS, *Palestinian Public Opinion Poll no. 44*, October 14–16, 1999.

21. For more detailed background and description of PLC members, see Barry Rubin, *The Transformation of Palestinian Politics: From Revolution to State-Building* (Cambridge, Mass.: Harvard University Press, 1999). Rubin presents a slightly different but not inconsistent characterization of PLC membership in his book.

22. Author interview with Rafiq al-Natshe, October 6, 1999.

23. PECDAR was established as an independent organization to both plan and channel foreign assistance dollars to Palestinian infrastructure development projects. PECDAR is said to be indirectly controlled by Ra'is Arafat.

24. Author interview with Mahmoud Labadi, October 16, 1999.

25. The NGO Law will be discussed in Chapter 4.

26. Labadi voiced the same opinion with regard to Arafat's nonreaction to the 1997 PA Corruption Report, a report that will be discussed below.

27. At times, it seems that Abu Ala is actually *part* of the executive authority. Abu Ala is, allegedly, a regular participant in Ra'is Arafat's "cabinet-plus" meetings, which include ministers as well as officials from the Palestinian security forces. He is also often a negotiator on the Israeli–Palestinian peace process track.

28. The most conspicuous examples of Abu Ala's policy have been the Basic Law and several of the budget laws.

29. See "al-Jalsa al-istithna'iyya lil-Majlis al-Tashre'i" [The Special Session of the PLC], *al-Majlis al-Tashre'i Shahriyya Natiqa bi-ism al-Majlis al-Tashre'i al-Falastini* [Palestinian Legislative Council Monthly], no. 4 (April 1998), p. 33.

30. See "al-Majlis al-Tashre'i al-Falastini: al-qararat" [The Decisions of the PLC], *al-Majlis al-Tashre'i Shahriyya*, no. 5 (1998), p. 43.

31. See Chapter 5 for a more complete discussion of USAID development work with the PLC.

32. Author interview with AbdelJawad Saleh, November 23, 1999. A hearing eventually took place at Baladna Cultural Center in al-Bireh, without the assistance of ARD or the blessing of Abu Ala.

33. Jaafer Sadqa, "Istiqalat lajnat al-muwazana fil-Tashre'i" [The PLC Budget Committee Resigns], *al-Ayyam*, November 15, 1999, online in Arabic at http://www.al-ayyam.com.

34. Author interview with Kamal Ash Sharafi, February 19, 1999. In addition to his disregard for the PLC, Arafat has been credited with preventing the establishment of an independent judiciary.

35. "PLC Report: PA Extorts Protection Money," Middle East News Line (MENL), November 15, 1999.

36. "Muqtatafat min al-taqrir . . . al-Sanawi al-awal lil-'aam 1996" [The PLC Special Committee Report Concerning the Annual Report of the General Comptroller Office for 1996], *al-Siyassa al-Filastiniyya* 4, nos. 15–16 (Summer–Autumn 1997), pp. 211–237.

37. These included Kamal Ash Sharafi, Hassan Kharesha, Hatim Abdel Qader, and Jamal Shati. The other five members of the Special Committee hailed from the Budget and Financial Affairs Committee.

38. "Muqtatafat min al-taqrir . . .," pp. 211–237.

39. As of December 1999, there were thirty cabinet ministries. The previous cabinet consisted of twenty-two members at the time it was reshuffled.

40. Abdallah Isa, "Interview with Brigadier General Musa Arafat," *al-Majallah*, December 20–26, 1998, in Foreign Broadcast Information Service–Near East and South Asia Daily Report (FBIS-NES-98-365), December 31, 1998.

41. ARD, "Performance Measurement Report no. 2" (draft), submitted to USAID/West Bank and Gaza, December 31, 1998.

42. Article 44, Basic Law.

43. Author interview with Hatim Abdul Qader, February 16, 1999.

44. Mohammed Daraghmeh, "Legislators Discuss Rights Violations with Nablus Audience," Associated Press (AP), August 12, 1996.

45. Imad Musa, "Human Rights Report Citing Improvements Sparks Controversy," AP Worldstream, March 29, 1998.

46. A translation of the petition, "A Cry from the Home Land," can be found on the Website of the Palestinian Human Rights Monitoring Group (PHRMG) at http://www.phrmg.org.

47. In an interview following the shooting, al-Masri said, "The PA knows

who shot me. . ."; see "Anti-Corruption Palestinians Defiant after Shooting," *Arabia Online*, December 2, 1999, available at http://www.arabia.com. Inexplicably, Palestinian police have refused to investigate the al-Masri incident. See "PA Refuses to Investigate Police in PLC Shooting," MENL, December 3, 1999.

Chapter 4

The PLC and Internal Palestinian Governance

Contrary to the prevailing perception, most of the work of the Palestinian Legislative Council (PLC) is focused on the business of internal Palestinian governance and not—as it might appear—on peace process issues. To be sure, there are lengthy and ongoing discussions on the floor of the PLC about Jerusalem, Palestinian refugees, and funding for families of "martyrs."[1] In terms of percentages, however, the vast majority of the council's time and effort is devoted to debating legislation, conducting oversight of the executive authority, and exploring issues crucial to the day-to-day affairs of the Palestinian Authority (PA). As with any parliament, most of these issues are rather mundane. On a typical day, for example, the PLC might discuss auto theft, labor laws, investment laws, education, unions, local elections, or even women and work. Some of the PLC's more significant endeavors have been efforts at bureaucratic reform and debate of the PA budget. It is this type of work that constitutes the mainstay of the council's legislative life.

Civil Service Law

Like the Basic Law, the complexities, complications, and impediments to the implementation of the PLC's Civil Service Law encapsulate the difficulties faced by the council since its inception. Conceived as a tool of good governance, the Civil Service Law was intended to systematize, regulate, and modernize the PA bureaucracy. The law establishes guidelines for uniform pay grades; standardizes qualifications for positions and titles; and creates procedures for performance reviews, hiring, and firing. It requires that government employees at the lowest salaries receive substantial raises, and it seeks to bring the salaries of civil administration and ministry employees onto the same pay scale. If properly implemented, the Civil Service Law could trim the bloated, top-heavy Palestinian bureaucracy.

By most accounts, such a law was sorely needed. The creation of the PA in 1994 and the establishment of a new governmental bureaucratic structure warped the salary scale and destroyed any sense of equanimity in the public sector.[2] PA executive authority employees were paid on an entirely different scale than were the former (Palestinian) employees of the Israeli-run Civil Administration, which the PA took over in 1994; this created a situation in which a teacher with twenty-five years of experience in the Civil Administration could earn less than a new teacher employed by the PA Ministry of Education.[3] The law was also designed to rectify the problem of PA salaries being linked to the Israeli shekel, and hence subject to periodic fluctuations in worth. Because of a devaluation of the shekel against the dollar, for example, PA employees paid in shekels saw their salaries lose nearly 25 percent of their value in 1998.[4]

Despite the concerted efforts of Palestinian legislators, the Civil Service Law has encountered one obstacle after another in its circuitous route to implementation. The law was initiated in draft form on the floor of the council in August 1996. After nearly five months of research, discussion, and debate, it passed its first reading on January 29, 1997. On June 3, 1997, the law passed its second reading and was forwarded to the *ra'is* (president), Yasir Arafat, for ratification. By October 1997, however, Arafat had neither signed the law nor published it in *al-Jarida al-Rasmiyya* (the *Official Gazette*). Consequently, during its October 27–29, 1997, session the PLC issued a decree demanding that the executive authority expedite implementation of the law. Arafat eventually ratified the law on May 28, 1998—nearly one year after it had been passed by the PLC.[5]

Top PA officials greeted the ratification of the Civil Service

Law with optimism. Marwan Barghouthi, PLC representative from Ramallah and leader of Fatah's West Bank *tanzim* (political party structure), welcomed Arafat's ratification as a "positive step" that "brings us [the PLC] closer to effecting administrative reform in the institutions and ministries of the PA."[6] Yet even after its ratification, implementing the Civil Service Law took months. A small but significant and noisy segment of executive authority beneficiaries—who feared demotions and the potential for slowed promotion—voiced strong opposition to the law, placing implementation on indefinite hold. Other critics of the law included Palestinian economists and analysts, some of whom criticized legislators for not analyzing the law's ramifications or having an understanding of its cost of implementation. While these critiques were to some degree accurate, it seems apparent—for reasons that will be discussed shortly—that the primary opponent to the implementation of the Civil Service Law was Arafat himself.

At first glance, it is difficult to understand how the Civil Service Law became the locus of such controversy. The law itself is straightforward if not a little ambiguous. In tedious fashion, the law discusses government holidays, vacation and sick days, the role of the *Diwan al-Muwazafin* (the Civil Service Bureau), the various classifications of employees, pay grades and raise schedules, disciplinary procedures for misconduct and poor job performance, and procedures for government appointments including the mandatory posting of position vacancies in two daily newspapers.[7] Most important, though, the Civil Service Law dared to address one of the more pressing issues of Palestinian governance: the conflict between *munadilin* (strugglers) and those with technically appropriate qualifications.[8] The munadilin, who served the Palestinian cause—both administratively and militarily—for years while residing at the Palestine Liberation Organization (PLO) headquarters in Tunis (and elsewhere outside of the West Bank and Gaza), had been awarded a disproportionate number of choice positions in the PA bureaucracy. These government positions represent job security in a depressed Palestinian economy and are therefore highly sought-after commodities. Ironically, PA hiring practices favoring munadilin had excluded and alienated many of the Palestinians who struggled during the *intifada* (uprising) from within what is currently PA-controlled territory. The appointments of munadilin entrenched Arafat's loyalists in the PA, engendering the resentment of much of the indigenous Palestinian population.

Two clauses of the Civil Service Law deal specifically with the dilemma of how appropriately to reward the munadilin for their service. In Article 107, the PLC attempted to correlate on-the-job work experience with less relevant, but perhaps equally esteemed, "revolutionary" credentials. The article states:

> Without prejudice to the provisions of this law, the Council of Ministries shall issue regulations that explain the rules for calculating the period of service or previous experience for employees at the PLO or its institutions or members of the resistance forces, liberated detainees and all those alike, and others who have served and had previous experience. It should be taken into consideration not to differentiate among those [who do] and those who [do] not benefit from this provision.[9]

Article 23 makes provisions for a specific percentage of PA positions to be allocated to munadilin:

> The Council of Ministries shall determine the allocation of a percentage of jobs to released prisoners and people injured in resistance operations whose condition allows them to perform the tasks under these jobs. In addition, the Council of Ministries shall determine a description of the aforementioned injured people and rules for their work in these jobs.
>
> In the case where injured people were completely disabled or died, then their spouses or sons or brothers or sisters supporting them can be appointed for these jobs, if they meet the required conditions.

The provisions of the second paragraph of Article 23 are applicable to families of martyrs. Part of the rationale for including these clauses in the law was to systematize and regulate the rampant nepotism that has characterized the PA bureaucracy. In recent years, the need to establish a framework within which to rein-in conspicuous favoritism had become acute. These clauses constitute the PLC's efforts to recognize and reconcile the legitimate sacrifices of the munadilin with the necessities dictated by a modern, efficient, and fair government bureaucracy.

By passing the Civil Service Law, Palestinian legislators did not intend to dismiss or undercut the "legitimate rights" of the strugglers. Rather, it seems that the law was designed to ensure that PA hiring practices would be more equitable for all. As one Palestinian economist pointed out, it is well understood and widely accepted that Arafat's style of rule requires that he be afforded 10 percent of hiring exceptions to put his "people" in positions. PLC legislators appear to be aware—and accepting—of this reality. The Civil Service Law merely constituted an attempt to level the playing field by limiting these exceptions and closing extensive loopholes in the system.

Implementation Crises

Although Arafat ratified the Civil Service Law in May 1998, as of autumn 1999, very little of the law had been implemented. When pressed for an explanation, the favored excuse among executive authority officials has been the "financial constraints" related to implementation. When the law was first conceived in 1995, there were only 22,000 employees in the PA Employee Bureau. By the end of 1998, there were more than 113,000.[10] In addition to covering all these PA civil servants, the law applies to all personnel in the security forces and staff of the PLO and its institutions.[11] Estimates vary widely as to how much it would cost to implement the law. According to Minister of Social Affairs Intisar al-Wazir (Um Jihad), the cost would be $43 million per month, or $516 million per year—a figure she maintained would "crush the budget."[12] Minister of Finance Muhammad Zuhair al-Nashashibi estimated the cost at 160 million shekels, or nearly $40 million, annually.[13] Minister of Industry Sa'adi al-Krunz, rapporteur of the ministerial committee charged with the Civil Service Law, estimated the cost to be $160 million per year.[14] Regardless, no allocation was made in the PA's fiscal year (FY) 1998 budget for expenditures associated with implementing the law, and FY99 was not much different. The initial FY99 draft budget submitted to the PLC by Finance Minister Nashashibi allocated only 1.67 million shekels—roughly $400,000—for the law's implementation.[15]

In November 1998, however, in the wake of a PA-wide teachers' strike, the executive did begin a phased implementation of the Civil Service Law through which teachers and some categories of civil servants received substantial pay increases—reportedly up to 45 percent. Shortly thereafter, Palestinian military employees began pressuring their commanders for their own salaries to be doubled—and threatened overt rebellion of the raises did not come through.[16] By mid-December, many of the extremely high initial raises were cut by 30 percent. A series of strikes followed, some of which protested for, and some against, the law's phased-in implementation. Doctors and pharmacists, for example, protested what they perceived as the negative ramifications of the law, while engineers went on strike because they believed that less-than-total abidance by the Civil Service Law hurt their own professional interests.[17] On January 6, 1999, judges in Gaza staged a one-hour strike to protest the salary cuts.[18] In a widely anticipated move on January 14, Arafat suspended the Civil Service Law altogether.

The next day, during an interview in the Palestinian daily *al-Hayat al-Jadida,* Minister of Industry al-Krunz suggested that Arafat had only the best intentions of fully implementing the law. He said, "Arafat is determined to completely implement the law in stages. The [p]resident has agreed to all the suggestions of the ministerial committee, but he asked to delay some of the clauses—he did not reject them."[19] Al-Krunz also assured Palestinians that the law would "not allow the decrease in salary of any employee."[20] Perhaps most important, however, al-Krunz emphatically stated the Civil Service Law would not "ignore" the munadilin. He said a committee had been established to study the strugglers' files, case by case. PLC secretary general Rawhi al-Fatouh echoed al-Krunz's assertions, saying the suspension of the law was only a temporary measure and that it would "be reactivated as soon as committees of specialized experts finish studying the loopholes in the law that could be unfair to the rights of the strugglers."[21] In January 1999, a PLC committee was formed to reconcile the details of how Clause 107 of the law—which concerns the munadilin—would be implemented.[22]

Arafat discussed the issue of the munadilin with Fatah officials as well as with trade unions and organizations. But ministry-level and Fatah party assurances regarding Arafat's sympathies and intentions apparently did not inspire much public confidence. In February 1999, another executive attempt at a phased implementation of the law was met with general strikes and large protests. Popular opinion among PA employees was divided concerning the law's implementation. Civil Administration employees with experience and qualifications—who clearly stood to benefit most from the law—were its most ardent supporters. Yet it remains unclear exactly what would happen to the munadilin, who constitute part of Arafat's main base of support. Promises have been made not to reduce any salaries, but at the same time, the law mandates the reduction of job titles to reflect the formal educational levels of employees. At the very least, implementation of the law would represent in many cases a demotion in occupational status for the munadilin.

The bottom line is that, although admittedly flawed, the Civil Service Law represents a concerted PLC effort to reform the PA administration. It grapples with difficult issues and overtly opposes executive will. Therefore, as with many other laws, and despite its ratification, the Civil Service Law continues to await implementation.

Budget Laws

Since the PLC's inception, one of its biggest sources of frustration has been the process of passing budget laws. As stipulated in *al-Nitham al-Dakhli* (the PLC Standing Orders), the Ministry of Finance must present the budget to the legislature by November 1, two months prior to the start of the new fiscal year.[23] The two-month lead time was intended to provide the PLC finance and budget committee and Palestinian legislators ample time to debate, discuss, and revise the budget. In what until recently was an annual tradition, however, the PA Ministry of Finance delivered the budgets to the legislature several months late in each of the legislature's first three years. This affront to legislative authority denied the PLC time to contemplate, study, and modify the budget before putting it to a vote. At the same time, this delay—and the lack of serious repercussions for the offending Finance Ministry—undercut the PLC's power and standing within the PA.

In a sense, the PLC's struggle to assert its legally sanctioned influence on the annual budget is a proxy war between Arafat and the legislature for financial control of the PA. After three years of this tug-of-war, the PLC has gained little ground. PLC dealings with the Ministry of Finance have been more difficult than those with other sectors of the executive authority, perhaps because Minister of Finance al-Nashashibi wears more than one hat. In addition to serving in Arafat's government, al-Nashashibi is the chairman of the Palestine National Fund, a Washington-based Palestinian fund-raising institution, and a member of the most powerful decision making body in Palestinian politics, the PLO Executive Committee. Al-Nashashibi, like most PA ministers, is a trusted ally of Arafat.

The annual budget brawls between the PLC and the Ministry of Finance have focused on a few major points of contention. Foremost among these are the aforementioned gratuitous delays in the annual PA Budget presentation to the PLC by Finance Minister al-Nashashibi. Moreover, all three budgets (1997–1999) that al-Nashashibi has presented to the PLC have contained gross inaccuracies—in particular, they have not reflected major sources of revenue generated by the PA. Additionally, the budgets have highlighted differences in philosophy between the Ministry of Finance and the PLC regarding what proportion of the budget should be allocated to the office of the ra'is and to the security apparati of the PA.

The frustration of PLC legislators with budget law procedures and the obstructionist behavior of the executive authority has resulted in an overtly hostile relationship between the legislature and al-Nashashibi. In fact, despite indications that Arafat has supported the Ministry of Finance in its violation of PLC Standing Orders, many PLC members hold al-Nashashibi personally responsible for the budget impasses of the past three years. Harsh critiques of the minister have been compounded by persistent reports of corruption and nepotism in the ministry.[24] Although several years have since passed, the appointment of al-Nashashibi's daughter to a top Finance Ministry position is still recalled with disdain at PLC headquarters in al-Bireh. Whereas most observers have dismissed the 1998 report published in *al-'Awda* magazine accusing al-Nashashibi of embezzling PA funds, his ministry's policies and his personal demeanor have made his conduct grist for the PLC's mill.[25] Yet, despite the personalized nature of this conflict, al-Nashashibi has emerged relatively unscathed. It is instructive here to review the origins and history of the PLC's budget difficulties.

The PLC versus the Ministry of Finance

Problems emerged between the Ministry of Finance and the PLC shortly after the legislature convened for its inaugural term in March 1996. Notably, the earliest disputes concerned the 1996 PA budget, which had been passed prior to the legislators' election. In May 1996 and again in June, the PLC requested that the Ministry of Finance present the 1996 budget to the legislature for review.[26] Apparently, disagreements regarding the appropriate level of cooperation between the PLC and the Finance Ministry were not resolved that summer, for during the September 11–12, 1996, session the council issued a resolution demanding that al-Nashashibi "cooperate with the [PLC Budget] Committee."[27]

Fiscal Year 1997

These difficulties carried over to the 1997 budget process. In October 1996—in preparation for the November 1 budget deadline—the PLC passed two resolutions requesting that the Ministry of Finance submit the 1997 budget to the legislature for review. One month later, during a mid-November interview, al-Nashashibi indicated that the budget was nearly complete and would be presented to the PLC "shortly." Even though the budget was already late, he added somewhat derisively that he hoped the PLC would be able to review and issue the budget law "before the end of this year."[28] Despite al-Nashashibi's optimistic November statement, the budget was not, in fact, delivered to the PLC prior to the new year. Anticipating this, in December 1996, the PLC passed a resolution requesting that al-Nashashibi appear before the council to clarify the reasons for the delay.[29] Al-Nashashibi did not attend, but he sent a letter saying that the budget was ready. Even so, the budget was not delivered. Two months later, in February 1997, the PLC threatened a no-confidence vote to remove the finance minister if he did not present the budget immediately.[30] On March 16, 1997—five months after the November 1996 deadline—al-Nashashibi finally delivered the 1997 budget to the PLC Budget Committee. Given the delay, the committee was, in effect, presented with a *fait accompli* and was forced to limit its review of the budget.

Briefly stated, the PLC budget review process is quite simple. The minister of finance, in coordination with the cabinet, creates a draft budget, which it then presents to the PLC Budget and Financial Affairs Committee for extensive review and comment. The committee then issues a detailed report, and the findings are discussed in a plenary session of the PLC. The report is then delivered to the Ministry of Finance and the Council of Ministers, which are required to respond (satisfactorily) to the committee report in short order.

In terms of the 1997 budget, the committee reviews, although abbreviated, nevertheless discovered serious flaws in the budget. The committee's investigative report, for example, noted that the "revenues" budget line item did not include proceeds from PA-owned monopolies, such as the General Commission for Petroleum, the Palestinian Society for Trade Services (i.e., the cement industry), and the General Commission for Tobacco. The report requested that the Finance Ministry "correct this and . . . channel all revenues, without exception, into the state coffers."[31] One Palestinian official confided that revenues from these monopolies accounted for more than $100 million per year—and constituted the difference between a PA budget surplus or deficit.[32]

Prior to approving the $866-million 1997 domestic operating budget, PLC members also debated and revised some specific line-item allocations. The legislature subtracted $8 million from the proposed budget of $248 million for the PA police forces. Likewise, the PLC Budget Committee recommended decreasing Arafat's office budget from 11 percent of the total budget (or roughly $95 million) to 8.5 percent ($75 million). No separate itemized budget was submitted for the expenditures of Arafat's office. Nevertheless, PLC Speaker Abu Ala rejected this controversial proposal to curtail the budget of the ra'is.[33] In response to this intervention by Abu Ala, one legislator, Azmi Shuyabi, threatened to resign.[34]

By the time the PLC voted on the budget, many legislators had lost their enthusiasm. Out of eighty-eight members, only sixty-four attended the session. Of these, thirty-six members voted for the budget, twenty-two voted against, and six abstained. The poor turnout for the vote—as well as the disappointment and frustration subsequently articulated by Budget Committee members—was probably indicative of PLC members' dissatisfaction with the process. Given the delay and the limited time to review and debate the budget, the PLC had been compelled to pass the law quickly. The 1997 Budget Law passed its first reading on May 27, 1997, and was ratified by Arafat on the same day. This set a bad precedent. By tolerating the excessive delay and making empty threats to vote no confidence, the PLC had effectively undermined its own power vis-à-vis the executive authority. Consequently, the council's threats against the executive lost their credibility. The morass of the 1997 budget process would therefore recur in 1998 and 1999.

Fiscal Year 1998

Except for a few notable events, the FY98 budget process encountered difficulties similar to the FY97 process. As with the 1997 budget, the FY98 budget missed the November 1 deadline. In a December 11, 1997, floor discussion about the 1998 budget, PLC members articulated what they perceived to be the significance of the budget process, which they described as "a tool in the hands of the PLC to supervise the performance and revise the policies of the executive authority."[35] Later that month, in preparation for another expected delay, Abu Ala proposed—at the suggestion of Arafat—a measure stipulating that expenditures be disbursed at a rate of one-twelfth of the previous year's budget per month until the new budget was passed. Arafat reportedly told Abu Ala that the budget would be ready by mid-January 1998.[36]

After months of PLC grumbling and executive authority stalling, al-Nashashibi eventually submitted the 1998 budget to the PLC on March 31, 1998. The Budget Committee reviewed it and sent it to the PLC for general discussion on April 28. A copy of the PLC Budget Committee report, complete with comments and questions, was delivered to the Council of Ministers at the end of April. But when the PLC still had not received any feedback from the ministers by May 11, the PLC resolved to convene a special session to discuss a vote of no confidence in the government.[37] On May 30, the PLC finally put its foot down and resolved to convene a special session on June 15 to discuss the 1998 budget as well as the "other problem of the relationship between the executive authority and the PLC, in light of discussions to vote to remove confidence in the government."[38]

Apparently this PLC resolution hit home with the executive. In one of the more bizarre turns of events in the short history of the PLC, Arafat responded to the May 30 PLC threat by writing a letter to PLC Speaker Abu Ala, asking the PLC to delay the special session for ten days to allow him enough time to form a new government and submit it to the PLC for approval. The PLC consented to Arafat's request and changed the date of the special session to June 25, 1998.[39] On that day, the PLC again postponed the special session until June 29. What happened between May 30 and June 29 is unclear, but on June 29, without a new government, the PLC confirmed the recommendations of the PLC Budget Committee and passed the 1998 PA General Budget.

The budget was only slightly higher than the previous year, coming in at $1.777 billion, with a $35 million deficit. This sum included a $877-million domestic operating budget—including $465 million in salary expenditures for PA employees—and $900 million in foreign donations.

Fiscal Year 1999

The 1999 budget continued what had become a three-year tradition of difficulties with the Ministry of Finance. As with previous years, November and December passed without any sign of the budget. In early January 1999, just prior to the week-long Muslim celebration of 'Eid al-Fitr, the PLC discussed the Ministry of Finance delay and severely criticized what it described as the executive authority's deliberate policy of "ignoring" the legislature and the law.[40]

Later that month, al-Nashashibi appeared before the PLC to answer members' questions. As in 1998, he blamed the PA cabinet for the delay, indicating that he had anticipated cabinet discussions would last just a few days, but the debate had actually lasted four months.[41] He also attributed the hold-up to problems with the draft civil service law, explaining that because exact figures were not known, it would be impossible to reflect accurately the cost of this law in the budget. PLC members used the question period to reiterate the importance of turning in the budget on time. Al-Nashashibi asked the PLC for twenty more days to submit the budget.

Following al-Nashashibi's questioning, Budget Committee chairman Azmi Shuyabi delivered his Committee report to the PLC.[42] Shuyabi said that the Civil Service Law was not responsible for the budget submission delay, and he criticized al-Nashashibi and the Finance Ministry for ignoring the PLC and its budget revisions. The withholding of the budget, he said, was a violation of the law and was indicative of a three-year-old pattern of denigrating and ignoring the PLC as an institution. Shuyabi's report pinned squarely on al-Nashashibi the responsibility for not implementing the Civil Service Law and for not responding to PLC requests for the final Ministry of Finance budget expenditure summaries from 1997 and 1998. Based on these findings, Shuyabi recommended that the PLC not consent to al-Nashashibi's request for an additional twenty days. Rather, the Budget Committee chairman suggested that the PLC proceed with a vote to revoke confidence in the finance minister and remove him from his cabinet ministry. This vote did not take place, however; the PLC instead granted the finance minister the twenty additional days he had requested to submit the budget. (The finance minister later commented that Shuyabi had no right to request a vote of no confidence, because he knew that al-Nashashibi had submitted the budget to the Council of Ministers—in accordance with the law—in November 1998.[43])

At it was, al-Nashashibi did not submit the budget within those twenty days. In late March, frustrated by the continued delay, the PLC met to discuss the issue of confidence in the government.[44] This time, it seemed that the PLC threat was credible: Abu Ala told the Palestinian leadership that he "couldn't hold off the legislators any longer."[45] On April 4—after a six-month delay—al-Nashashibi submitted the 1999 budget to the council.

The budget submitted was $1.74 billion, including $693 million in foreign-funded development projects and a $896-million domestic operating budget; the anticipated deficit was $153 million.[46] Budget Committee chair Shuyabi said the study of the budget would take a month or two, and that the committee would make a number of suggestions to the PLC, the first of which, he assured, "would be to hold the Ministry of Finance responsible for the delay in submitting the budget, and the financial complications which resulted in causing this delay."[47]

In June 1999, just as it appeared that the budget saga had ended, the executive authority rekindled the issue.[48] During the week of June 13, the executive authority inexplicably demanded that members of the PLC Budget Committee—who had just completed the process of reviewing the 1999 budget but had not held a PLC plenary session discussion—return all copies of the document to the Ministry of Finance. One insider who had seen the budget related that it possessed "a striking lack of detail" and "read more like a budget summary than a detailed budget." Although not made public, the Budget Committee report was said to have been scathing. In a lengthy interview with the Palestinian daily *al-Hayat al-Jadida* on June 21, Shuyabi candidly discussed some of the more glaring deficiencies in the proposed budget.[49] In general, he was most critical of the lack of accountability.

During the interview, Shuyabi hinted at the content of the report submitted to the Council of Ministers. Individual ministries in the PA, he said, did not provide detailed budgets that included descriptions of requests, justifications for projected expenditures, or even accurate lists of payroll expenditures. By way of example, Shuyabi cited the Ministry of Tourism, a ministry with 385 employees on the payroll. When asked to provide the Finance and Budget Committee with a list of names and positions, the ministry could only come up with 258; no one could identify nearly one-third of the "employees" on the tourism payroll. "It is," said Shuyabi, "like this in all of the Ministries."[50] The problem of "ghost" employees is just one symptom of many related to the explosion in the overall PA payroll—which now includes about 120,000 persons.

In August 1999, the Ministry of Finance returned the revised budget to the PLC. The PLC subsequently met in plenary session and Shuyabi presented the findings of his committee's report. Among the highlights were that the Ministry of Finance had understated PA revenues. Several income-generating sources, either fully or partially controlled by the PA, were not taken into account in the budget. Among the profitable entities not listed were: the Palestinian Broadcasting Corporation, the Ministry of Housing, the Palestinian

Aviation Authority, the Central Bureau of Statistics, the Cigarettes Authority, the Energy Authority, the Petroleum Authority, the Monetary Authority, and the Water Authority.[51] The report also expressed concern over PA expenditures on automobiles.[52] Excluding the security forces, various ministries own 2,000 cars, costing the PA nearly 50 million shekels ($12.5 million) per year.[53]

In addition to citing corruption and lack of accountability, the budget report discussed what the committee obviously considered an alarming trend in PA budget priorities: a decrease in allocations for health and education, and a corresponding increase in the budget provisions for security and for the Ministry of the Interior—whose purview also encompasses security-related matters. Whereas in 1996 approximately 24 percent of the total PA budget was allocated to health and education, these sectors combined for only 12 percent of the total budget allocation in 1999. At the same time, the budget for the Interior Ministry and for security reached 37 percent. The committee called for a decrease in the budget and a reduction in the budget deficit.

After a very brief review, and with little fanfare, on August 12 the PLC passed the 1999 budget of 6.9 billion shekels ($1.7 billion) by a vote of thirty-eight to eighteen.[54] The budget that was returned to the PLC was somewhat revised: to reduce the deficit, funds were subtracted from a Ministry of Education line item. At the same time, an additional 95 million shekels were added to the security budget, bringing it up to 250 million shekels, or roughly $63 million. A deficit of $126 million remained.

Even as the 1999 budget passed the PLC, Shuyabi maintained that the issue was not entirely resolved. The committee demanded a meeting with the PA treasury to ensure that more of their suggested changes would be incorporated into the FY99 budget. During the last session of the period, the Finance and Budget Committee resolved to meet when the council reconvened on on October 14, 1999, to revisit the 1999 budget and discuss both the issue of reforming the Ministry of Finance and the firing of the minister of finance.[55]

The October 14 meeting did not occur until mid-November, when the plenary session was convened on November 14, ostensibly to discuss the 1999 and 2000 budgets and the status of the minister and Ministry of Finance. During the meeting, Shuyabi and the other budget committee members resigned *en masse* to protest Abu Ala's role in preventing the committee from carrying out its mandated role in the budget review process.[56] Shuyabi explained the resignation as follows:

> We don't see a justification for the presence of a budget committee that is not capable of undertaking its role in supervising the financial procedures of the government in conformity with the law.[57]

Two days later, the entire budget committee—with the exception of Shuyabi—withdrew their resignations, and the PLC reconvened. That day, November 17, in an unprecedented move, al-Nashashibi presented the FY2000 budget on time to the PLC. The FY2000 budget totaled nearly $1.4 billion; it included a $940-million domestic operating budget and $424 million for development spending.[58]

1999 PA Budget (all figures in millions)

1. General Revenues	
a. Domestic Revenues	$903.8
b. Foreign Aid to Finance Assistance Projects	$700.0
Total General Revenues	$1603.8
2. General Expenditures	
a. Current Expenditures	$990.2
b. Budget-Financed Capital Expenditures	$19.2
c. Development Expenditures	$720.0
Total General Expenditures*	$1729.5
3. Deficit (Expenditures less Revenues)	**$125.7**

Note: Figures are rounded.
Source: Mashru' qanun al-muwazana al-'ama lil-sana al-maliyya 1999 *(Palestinian General Budget Law for FY1999) PA Ministry of Finance, General Budget Department, July 1999.*

The budget struggle provides an interesting perspective into the conflicts between the executive authority and the PLC. Many in the PLC consider the Minister of Finance to be both personally and professionally responsible for the political confrontations between the ministry and the legislature. But it is not at all apparent that al-Nashashibi was, in fact, the primary obstruction. Many Palestinians—including both citizens and legislators—believe that al-Nashashibi merely acted as a proxy, implementing Arafat's will. Even though the finance minister is a member of the PLO Executive Committee and wields a significant amount of power in the Palestinian political bureaucracy, he is still widely perceived as being a role player and only a marginal decision maker in the budget conflict. The decision to delay the budget, most believe, was Arafat's alone. Because of this dynamic, behind closed doors many legislators describe al-Nashashibi as *maskin* (pitiful).

The NGO Law

The PLC's role in legislating *Qanun al-Jam'iyyat al-Khayriyya wa-al-Hay'at al-Ijtima'iyya* (the Law of Charitable Associations and Community Organizations) was noteworthy in the legislature's development. Better known as the Nongovernmental Organization (NGO) Law, this piece of legislation drew the ire of the Palestinian NGO community when the Council of Ministers initiated it in October 1997. Advocates of Palestinian democracy considered the law to be "very restrictive"; other advocates of Palestinian democracy portrayed it as a blatant effort by the PA executive to rein in the freedoms of Palestinian civil society.[59]

By way of background, the PA executive in 1994 set about to dismantle Palestinian NGOs and other voluntary organizations under its jurisdiction that it perceived to be impediments to state building.[60] Since then, Palestinian NGOs have considered themselves under siege. As part of this campaign, the PA managed to curtail funding to NGOs substantially by compelling international donors to funnel donations through the PA financial structure.[61] Critics of the PA understood the law as another in a series of PA bureaucratic tactics designed specifically to undercut and weaken the already reeling Palestinian NGO sector. But Palestinian officials such as Hasan Abdel Rahman, the PLO representative in Washington, routinely deny these accusations, maintaining that the Palestinian NGO Law is comparable to Private Voluntary Organization (PVO) laws in Western countries. At the same time, PA officials whisper that the legislation is necessary to constrain direct overseas funding of the many NGOs that they suspect are fronts for Hamas. Even so, the primary official PA criticism of the NGOs is that they are corrupt. In June 1999, PA minister of justice Freih Abu Meddien described the directors of local NGOs as "fat cats whose job is to distort and discredit the PA. . . . Their role in Palestinian society should be re-examined."[62]

Perhaps not surprisingly given its design, the draft NGO law contained a number of articles that alarmed the Palestinian NGO community. In particular, Palestinians working with local NGOs were disheartened by articles dealing with the NGO "registration" procedures. By compelling all NGOs to obtain the approval of the minister of justice, the law seemed to imply "licensure" rather than registration.[63] After the draft law was initiated, NGO leaders mobilized and formed a coalition of organizations to lobby PLC legislators to change the draft law. Generally speaking, this coalition sought a law that would afford more independence and less executive authority control over NGOs. The lobbying process was effective, and the changes that resulted from these efforts (which were reflected in the final draft of the NGO law) represented a healthy precedent for the functioning of Palestinian parliamentary democracy.

Starting in October 1997, and over the course of the next several months, workshops and town hall meetings were held during which NGO leaders and PLC members discussed specifics of the law, including perceived deficiencies and proposed changes. Heads of prominent NGOs met with Palestinian legislators in the halls of the PLC in al-Bireh and in home district offices. During these months, Mustafa Barghouthi, head of a prominent Ramallah-based NGO, purportedly met with more than seventy-five PLC members. By the time the law passed the PLC's third reading in December 1998, one director of a leading Palestinian NGO privately boasted that the law had undergone a 95 percent revision.[64]

At that point, the Palestinian NGO community was, by and large, satisfied with the status of the draft NGO law. At least disaster had been temporarily averted. Even so, the law faced the final hurdle of acquiring Arafat's approval. This too would prove an uphill battle. At the last moment, Arafat refused to sign the law because it required that NGOs register with the Ministry of Justice. Instead, Arafat maintained that the law should be modified so that NGOs would register with the Ministry of the Interior—headed by Arafat himself.[65] Although the terms of this modification were supported by the minister of justice, they were considered unacceptable to the NGO community.[66]

Once again, the NGO lobby coalition mobilized. This time, the coalition held a workshop attended by hundreds, during which a memorandum was drafted and signed by about 500 NGO leaders. The memo was later delivered to PLC members. In a subsequent vote in the PLC on May 25, thirty-eight members voted to retain the Ministry of Justice as the responsible agency while only twelve members—mostly cabinet ministers—voted to change the law to further empower Arafat's Interior Ministry. This vote constituted one of the few direct legislative rebuffs of Arafat since the PLC's establishment. Barghouthi, who worked long and hard to oppose Arafat's proposed changes to the already passed PLC law, described the vote as "a small victory." Still, he said, it was "a very important one."[67]

The law awaited Arafat's ratification and approval for publication in the *Official Gazette*. Several weeks later, however, the law still had not been signed. Then, on August 12, as PLC members were filing out from the final session of the legislative term, PLC Speaker Abu Ala read a letter from the Legal Committee that effectively invalidated the May 25 vote. The letter stated that the vote overriding the ra'is did not meet vote quorum requirements (for an absolute majority) designated by PLC Standing Orders. Article 71 of the Standing Orders stipulates that if the ra'is returns a law with comments, or with "justification for his rejection," the PLC shall re-discuss the law, and "then, if the draft law has been ratified by an absolute majority of the Council, it shall be considered law. . ." Accordingly, despite the vote results, the draft NGO law that included Arafat's changes—that is, the one in which registration procedures are handled through the Ministry of the Interior—would become law.[68]

The legal basis for this decision was, and continues to be, a subject of controversy in the PLC. Article 71(b) of the Standing Orders is vague, and it is unclear whether proper procedure dictates that an absolute majority of the PLC is required to ratify or to veto the changes suggested by the ra'is. In this case, the PLC voted against Arafat's suggested changes, voting instead to ratify the previous version of the law. No vote was taken to ratify Arafat's suggested changes.

Many legislators were said to be demoralized by this surprising turn of events. Given the prevailing morale after this latest defeat, it did not appear that the legislators would continue to push the issue. Political Committee chair Ziad Abu-Amr perhaps said it best when he described the situation: "People," he said, "got tired."[69]

Political Parties Law

In September 1995, the *Diwan al-Fatwa wa-al-Tashre'i*, a legislative bureau in the PA Ministry of Justice, published a draft *Qanun al-'Ahzab al-Siyasiyya* (political parties law). This draft law was roundly criticized by observers and prodemocracy NGOs as highly restrictive and antidemocratic.[70] At the time, it appeared that the executive authority intended to pass and implement the law in preparation for the first ever PA elections, slated for January 1996. The draft law as promulgated by the Diwan al-Fatwa never passed, but discussion of the law reemerged in January 1997 as the PLC initiated its own draft legislation to regulate political parties. As of late 1999, the draft political parties law had progressed no further than general discussion.

A main criticism of the 1995 draft law was that it did not create an atmosphere conducive to the development of political pluralism and democracy. The draft law established a committee structure that consisted of high-ranking PA officials and executive authority appointees tasked with "registering" political parties. This committee was endowed with the legal authority to accept, reject, ban, or otherwise penalize parties based on a number of subjective criteria. An application for registration could be rejected, for example, if the party platform or its activities—or both—were judged to "contravene the provisions of the constitution, the bases of national unity, and overall peace."[71] In addition to the broad latitude afforded to this committee, the law contained a number of other stringent monitoring mechanisms whereby parties would be obligated to report the names of their members, activities, and funding sources to the PA. Essentially, the law made all parties accountable to the PA, which is run by the PLO—the dominant force in Palestinian politics. If passed, this law would have legally mandated the proverbial fox guarding the hen house.

The 1997 PLC draft legislation proposed by the PA cabinet did appear to correct some of the weaknesses of the earlier draft law, but it is still clear that the 1995 draft constituted the starting point and basis of the 1997 legislation. A major revision in the 1997 draft was the replacement of the "Registration Committee" with the Ministry of Justice. The Ministry of Justice would henceforth play the role of judge and jury in determining the suitability of political party applicants. In the PA, which lacks an independent judiciary, this may be a distinction without a difference. In terms of good legislation, however, it was certainly a welcome change.

Despite these changes, the 1997 draft Political Party Law remained controversial. Article 2 of the 1997 draft, for example, states that "the political system in Palestine is based on the principles defined in the Basic Law, and on the principles of political pluralism and the freedom to form parties."[72] This optimistic statement belies the content of much of the legislation that follows, which neither encourages political pluralism nor ensures the right to form parties. As with the 1995 draft law, the 1997 version defines parties that threaten the "unity of the country" as well as "regional and societal unity" as unwelcome. Likewise, in the new draft law, the Ministry of Justice retains the right to refuse to register a political party; Articles 15 and 16 describe a "registration" procedure and a process to appeal a decision of the Ministry of Justice in cases of rejection.

One of the distinguishing characteristics of the 1997 draft law is that it stipulates PA funding for political parties. In Article 21, the PA commits financial assistance—a line item from the annual budget—to political parties that participated in the last elections. Funds are provided to parties based on the percentage of seats obtained (with a 2 percent threshold). Although this law has not yet been passed, a similar practice is already in use by the PA. Leaving aside the question of how much PA money is channeled to the PLO, smaller parties—like *al-Haraka al-Wataniyya lil-Taghir* (the National Movement for Change, or NMC)—currently receive funding directly from the PA.

The NMC has received PA political party funding for nearly three years. Yet, according to Khader el-Moghrabi, secretary general of the NMC, receiving PA funding is not without its disadvantages. For example, el-Moghrabi reported that his party once had twelve offices in Gaza. Because of funding difficulties, however, the party had been forced to close six of them. The problem, lamented el-Moghrabi, was Arafat: "Sometimes he delivers [funding], and sometimes he doesn't."[73] In contrast to the NMC, the Gaza-based and Hamas-affiliated political party *Hizb al-Khalas* (Party of Redemption) does not receive PA funding. Shaykh Ahmad al-Bahar, president of the party's consultative council, was well aware that Hizb al-Khalas—a registered political party like the NMC—should be entitled to money from the PA. When asked why his party wasn't receiving PA funds, al-Bahar laughed and feigned ignorance: "I don't know," he said. "Why don't you go ask Arafat?"[74]

Miscellaneous Oversight Work

In addition to legislative work focused on governance issues, the PLC also devotes a substantial amount of time to oversight issues related to the everyday affairs of the PA. In general terms, the PLC routinely discusses and debates the merits of topics such as customs tariffs, environmental protections, automobile registration problems, traffic laws, and factory safety codes. Education is also a highly discussed topic in the PLC, which often debates the state of university and higher education in the PA. Likewise, the declining quality of healthcare in the PA is a regular topic on the PLC agenda.

The PLC schedule also touches on other significant issues. In October 1998, for example, the council had a floor debate about what should be done on May 4, 1999, the final day of the transitional period as defined by the Oslo accords. On occasion, the PLC also reviews and ratifies decisions of the executive. On May 12, 1999, the PLC ratified the terms of a loan agreement between the PA and the Kuwait-based Arab Fund for Economic and Social Development, to fund a rural development project.[75] (See Appendix IV.) It is unclear whether this exercise of authority is a stipulated PLC responsibility or is merely an accepted practice.

To better inform the discussions and floor debates, ministers and executive authority officials are periodically requested to attend legislative hearings. For a hearing dealing with land boundry registration, the PLC requested that the ministers of justice, housing, and local government attend a session to answer the questions of PLC members.[76] In fact, PA minister of local government Sa'eb Erekat has appeared before the PLC several times. Erekat's appearances provide a good example of the range of questions directed at PA ministers. (He is also one of the few ministers who actually appears before the PLC when requested.) During one session in 1997, Erekat answered questions about local licenses required by businessmen and investors doing business in the PA. In another session that year, he was asked to discuss the legal procedures employed by the PA to expropriate Palestinian land for an industrial zone near Nablus.

Questions directed toward ministers do, at times, provide insight into important societal conflicts in the PA. In an unusual exchange that took place in November 1997, Jamal Shubaki, a legislator from Hebron, queried Erekat about the role of the *mukhtar* (traditional village chief) within the Palestinian legal system.[77] Al-Shubaki asked Erekat about the duties of the mukhtar, and whether it would be preferable to have both a mukhtar and a local (i.e., PA) government. The question encapsulated the dilemma posed when the modern state system interacts with traditional society.[78] In short, Erekat answered that, by bringing a legitimacy not carried by local government, the mukhtar can continue to play a useful role coexisting with the PA local government. Erekat indicated that he was considering formalizing the role of the mukhtar in legislation.

On April 15, 1998, Erekat found himself answering a less profound question. That day, he faced hostile questioning by twenty-five PLC members focusing on why he had not implemented the Local Elections Law and held local elections in Tulkarm. Nearly a year and a half earlier, in December 1996, the law had been passed by the PLC and ratified by Arafat. As it stood, the mayor and local council of Tulkarm had been appointed by Arafat. Earlier that April, however, the PLC had appointed a local election council to start the necessary procedures for holding local elections in the city. This committee—which presumably fell under the jurisdiction of Erekat—was dismissed. Hassan Kharesha, a legislator from Tulkarm, was particularly pointed in his questions to Erekat, who responded that he could provide documents to the PLC detailing exactly what occurred in Tulkarm, and pledged that the PA would hold elections at the first possible opportunity.[79]

Conclusion

From discussions about mukhtars to automobile registration procedures, the business of the PLC is indeed wide ranging. As a state in the making, it is not surprising that the PA requires legislation. When the legislature started work in 1996, the legal environment of the PA was desolate, for upon his return to Gaza in 1994, Arafat had decreed all laws established during the thirty years of Israeli Civil Administration null and void. Legislators are acutely aware of the need to establish a legislative framework for the PA, and although they have lacked skills, they have largely taken their responsibilities seriously.

In the four years between 1996 and 2000, the PLC has worked on roughly sixty laws. (See Appendix V.) Among other topics, these laws have focused on economics, education, healthcare, prisons, labor, and agriculture. Legislators have also worked on a natural resources protection law, and have passed a Bar Association law to establish standards for the legal profession. On a more obscure front, in 1997 and 1998, the PLC worked on a veterinarians law, and a law regulating the citrus industry.

PLC members consider their legislative duties to be important, but often tedious, work. In contrast to their legislative efforts, PLC members appear to pursue their executive oversight duties with alacrity. Many of the oversight tasks are also mundane, but others—depending on the subject matter—are more appealing. Given the relationship with the executive, it is perhaps not surprising that some legislators relish the opportunity to exert power over the executive authority cabinet ministers or security officials. Still, the vast majority of the time, Palestinian legislators have remained focused on the issues at hand. Primarily, these issues relate to improving the nature of Palestinian governance.

Notes

1. See PLC Resolution 3/10/305, July 28, 1998. The PLC has periodically discussed the Support for Families of Martyrs, Prisoners of War, and Injured draft law since it was initiated in September 1997.

2. Prior to the establishment of the PA, an Israeli-run Civil Administration staffed with Palestinian employees constituted the Palestinian civil service bureaucracy. In 1994, the PA took over the Israeli Civil Administration and created an executive authority and a ministerial bureaucracy.

3. Author interview with Ghania Malhis, director, Palestine Economic Policy Research Institute (MAS), February 14, 1999.

4. Kamal Qubaysi, "Security Units Near Rebellion cver Wages," *al-Sharq al-Awsat*, November 18, 1998, in Foreign Broadcast Information Service (FBIS)–Near East and South Asia (FBIS-NES-98-322), November 18, 1998. The PLC called an emergency meeting with Finance Minister Muhammad Zuhair al-Nashashibi to discuss the effects of the devalued shekel on Palestinian society, and particularly the effect on PA employees paid in shekels.

5. See "al-Majlis al-Tashre'i al-Falastini: al-qararat" [The Decisions of the PLC], *al-Majlis al-Tashre'i Shahriyya Natiqa bi-ism al-Majlis al-Tashre'i al-Falastini* [Palestinian Legislative Council Monthly], no. 1 (January 1998), pp. 32–33.

6. Ali al-Salih, "West Bank: Sources Expect 'Formal' PA Cabinet Changes," *al-Sharq al-Awsat,* June 17, 1998, in FBIS-NES-98-168, June 18, 1998.

7. Concerning employee classifications, section 2, chapter 1 of the law designates the following classifications: special category—heads of governmental departments appointed as ministers; first category—doctors, engineers, legal, financial, etc., and professionals in supervisory roles; third category—technical and clerical jobs as well as secretarial and administrative services; fourth category—professional jobs dealing with electrical workshops and power stations; fifth category—service jobs such as guards, messengers, and others.

8. The Arabic term *munadil* literally means fighter, combatant, or defender; see Hans Wehr, *A Dictionary of Modern Standard Arabic* (Ithaca, N.Y.: Spoken Language Services, 1976).

9. An unofficial translation of the Civil Service Law was provided by Associates for Rural Development, a USAID contractor working with the PLC in Ramallah. The Arabic language copy is available on the Palestinian Legislative Council Website, http://www.pal-plc.org.

10. Na'el Musa, "'Ijma'a 'ala rafd tajmid Qanun al-Khidma al-Wataniyya" [Consensus not to freeze the Civil Service Law], *al-Hayat al-Jadida*, January 24, 1999, online in Arabic at http://www.alhayat-j.com.

11. The Civil Service Law is atypical of PA laws, as it is one of the few laws—if not the only one—that attempts to legislate for the PLO.

12. Author interview with Intisar al-Wazir, February 18, 1999.

13. Muneer Abu-Rizq, "Abu Shari'a: awamir ra'isiyya bi-ziyyadat rawatib jam'iyyat al-muwazafin" [Abu Shari'a: Presidential Decree to Increase Salaries], *al-Hayat al-Jadida* online in Arabic, January 29, 1999.

14. Minister of Industry Sa'adi al-Krunz, as quoted in Muneer Abu-Rizq, "al-Krunz: al-qanun la yasmah bi-takfid ratib 'ay muwazaf bal yamnahuhu 'alawat" [The Law Does Not Allow a Decrease in Employees' Salaries], *al-Hayat al-Jadida* online in Arabic, January 14, 1999.

15. Husam Izz al-Din, "PA Finance Minister Reports Budget Details to PLC," *al-Ayyam,* April 6, 1999, in FBIS-NES-1999-0413, April 14, 1999. Later drafts of the budget allocated $42.5 million for the partial implementation of the law; see "Mashru' qanun al-muwazana al-'ama lil-sana al-maliyya 1999" [The Palestinian General Budget Law for FY 1999], July 1999, available in Arabic by request from the PLC.

16. Ali al-Salih, "West Bank: Sources Expect 'Formal' PA Cabinet Changes," *al-Sharq al-Awsat,* June 17, 1998, in FBIS-NES-98-168, June 18, 1998. Although raises were not forthcoming, there was no overt rebellion.

17. Muneer Abu-Rizq, "West Bank and Gaza Strip: Gaza Paper Calls for Amending Civil Laws," *al-Hayat al-Jadida,* January 15, 1999, in FBIS-NES-99-020, January 22, 1999.

18. "PCHR Calls on the PA for the Full Implementation of the Civil Service Law," press release from *al-Markaz al-Falastini li-huquq al-'Insan* (Palestinian Center for Human Rights [PCHR]), January 25, 1999.

19. Abu-Rizq, "al-Krunz: al-qanun la yasmah bi-takfid ratib 'ay muwazaf bal yamnahuhu 'alawat."

20. Ibid.

21. Abu-Rizq, "West Bank and Gaza Strip: Gaza Paper Calls for Amending Civil Laws."

22. Muneer Abu-Rizq, "Diwan al-muwazafin injaz kabir fi zul al-tahadiyyat al-dakhiliyya wa-al-kharijiyya" [Employee Bureau: A Big Accomplishment in the Shadow of Internal and External Challenges], *al-Hayat al-Jadida* online in Arabic, February 1, 1999.

23. See *al-Nitham al-Dakhli* [Standing Orders], Article 68. Provided by the Parliamentary Research Unit (PRU), February 14, 1999.

24. For example, al-Nashashibi is said to have signature authority (with Muhammad Rashid) on one of Arafat's slush fund bank accounts in Israel known as *al-sunduq al-thani,* or the "second account." For more on this, see Ronen Bergman and David Ratner, "The Man Who Swallowed Gaza," *Ha'aretz* English supplement, April 4, 1997.

25. Yasir Arafat's mother-in-law, Raymonda Tawil, is the owner of *al-'Awda* magazine. Tawil accused al-Nashashibi of embezzling PA funds after

the Ministry of Finance withheld a subsidy of LE 10,000 (Egyptian pounds) per month from the magazine.

26. PLC Resolution 1/4/26, passed May 8–9, 1996. In the second request, the PLC also requested a copy of the 1995 PA budget. PLC Resolution 1/7/45, passed June 5–6, 1996. The PLC reiterated this request on June 20, 1996, with PLC Resolution 1/9/59 (passed June 20, 1996).
27. PLC Resolution 1/22/99, passed September 11–12, 1996.
28. "Palestinian Finance Minister Comments on Investment, Capital Fight," *al-Ayyam*, November 17, 1997, BBC Summary of World Broadcasts, November 25, 1999.
29. PLC Resolution 1/30/134, passed December 12, 1996.
30. PCHR, *al-Majlis al-Tashre'i al-Falastini* (Gaza City: PCHR, November 1998), p. 56.
31. "Arafat's Palestine: Closure, Corruption and Poverty," *Swiss Review of World Affairs*, September 1, 1997.
32. The deficit in the 1997 budget was $52 million.
33. Wafa Amr, "Palestinian Lawmakers Pass Arafat's Budget," Reuters, May 27, 1997. The legal and procedural basis for Abu Ala's refusal of the Budget Committee recommendation is unclear.
34. Arafat's office budget was not reduced, but Shuyabi did not resign; he later became chairman of the Budget Committee.
35. See "al-Jalsa al-thalitha wa-al-'ashrun lil-Majlis al-Tashre'i" [The Twenty-Third Session of the Legislative Council], *al-Majlis al-Tashre'i Shahriyya*, no. 2 (February 1998), p. 23.
36. Ibid., p. 29.
37. PLC Resolution 3/6/269, passed May 11, 1999.
38. PLC Resolution 3/7/282, passed May 30, 1998.
39. PLC Resolution 3/i4/289, passed June 15, 1998.
40. Muhammad Abu Khaddir, "al-Majlis al-Tashre'i qarara takhsis jalsat al-khamis li-munaqashat qadaya al-mu'ataqalin," [The PLC Decides to Convene a Special Session to Discuss the Issue of Prisoners], *al-Quds*, January 7, 1999, online in Arabic at http://www.alquds.com. During that session, the PLC also decided to establish a special committee to investigate reports that Arafat had decided to purchase new $100,000 BMWs for each member of his cabinet. "Jalsa khasa al yawm

li-munaqashat taqrir lajnat al-raqaba al-'ama al-khasa bil-mu'taqalin al-siyasiyyin" [Special Session Today to Discuss the Report of the Oversight Committee. . .], *al-Hayat al-Jadida* online in Arabic, January 8, 1999.

41. Abu-Rizq, "Abu Shari'a: awamir ra'isiyya bi-ziyyadat rawatib jam'iyyat al-muwazafin."

42. Ibid.

43. See "al-Nashashibi yarfud intiqad ba'd al-nuwab bi-sh'an taqdim al-mizaniyya" [al-Nashashibi Refuses Criticisms made by PLC Members Regarding Submitting the Budget], *al-Hayat al-Jadida* online in Arabic, March 18, 1999.

44. Husam Izz al-Din and Fayez Abu A'on, "Wazir al-maliyya ya'red amam al-Tashre'i al-yawm mashru' al-muwazana li-'aam 1999" [Minister of Finance Submits the 1999 Budget to the PLC], *al-Ayyam,* April 4, 1999, online in Arabic at http://www.al-ayyam.com.

45. Daoud Kuttab, "The Palestinian Budget," *Jerusalem Post,* April 8, 1999.

46. "Normal Times Help Stir Some Growth," *Middle East Economic Digest,* July 16, 1999, p. 9.

47. Izz al-Din and Abu A'on, "Wazir al-maliyya ya'red amam al-Tashre'i al-yawm."

48. In addition to its problems with the budget, during the summer of 1999, the Ministry of Finance was also under fire for its role in an ongoing crisis in the healthcare sector. See Na'el Musa, "al-Tashre'i yqar 'aliyyat li-mas'alat al-muraj'at al-mas'ula 'an 'amal al-'ajhiza al-'amniyya" [The PLC Decides on the Mechanism of Responsibility for the Work of the Security Apparatus], *al-Hayat al-Jadida* online in Arabic, June 24, 1999.

49. See "al-Na'ib al-Shuyabi yukshif tafasil asbab suhbat qanun al-muwazana min al-Majlis al-Tashre'i" [Minister Shuyabi Discloses Details of the Reasons Why the Budget Law Was Withdrawn from the PLC], *al-Hayat al-Jadida* (in Arabic), local events section, June 21, 1999.

50. Ibid.

51. Maher Abukhater, "1999 Budget Approved, Despite Strong Reservations," *Jerusalem Times,* August 20, 1999.

52. In August, PLC members discussed the formation of a committee to investigate the over-expenditure on automobiles in the ministries. See Husam Izz al-Din, "Thamaniyya wa thalathin na'ib yusawatun li-salih

iqrar muwazanat al-'aam 1999" [Thirty-eight Members Vote in Favor of the 1999 Budget], *al-Ayyam* online in Arabic, August 13, 1999.

53. Abukhater, "1999 Budget Approved."

54. Na'el Musa, "al-Tashre'i yqar al-muwazana al-'aam lil-sulta [The PLC Passes the General PA Budget], *al-Hayat al-Jadida* online in Arabic, August 14, 1999.

55. Ibid.

56. Jafer Sadiqa, "Istiqalat lajnat al-muwazana fil-Tashre'i bi-sabab khilafat bsh'an muwaznat al-'aam al-madi" [The Budget Committee in the PLC Resigns over Differences about Last Year's Budget], *al-Ayyam* online in Arabic.

57. Ibid.

58. Muhammed Abu Khudayr, "2000 General Budget Submitted by the PA Finance Minister," *al-Quds*, November 18, 1999, FBIS-NES-1999-1120.

59. Author interview with Mustafa Barghouthi, February 17, 1999. By coincidence, while the Palestinian NGO law was undergoing its final reading, the Egyptian government concurrently passed its own, highly restrictive and controversial NGO law. The Egyptian law appeared designed to curtail the growing power of Islamist elements in its own NGO sector.

60. Mehran Kamrava, "What Stands Between the Palestinians and Democracy," *Middle East Quarterly* 6, no. 2 (June 1999), pp. 3–12.

61. Ibid.

62. "Israelis Oppose PA Ruling on NGOs," Middle East News Line (MENL), June 15, 1999.

63. For a more detailed assessment of this law, see PCHR, *Critical Comments on the Draft Law of Charitable Associations and Community Organizations* (Gaza City: PCHR, November 1998).

64. Other efforts to lobby the legislature have not met with such impressive results. Rasem al-Bayari, Gaza president of the Palestine General Federation of Trade Unions, said his organization began to lobby the PLO in Tunis in the early 1990s to influence the text of the Palestinian labor law (which is currently in draft form). Despite concerted efforts, al-Bayari complained, the initial drafts of the labor law did not take into account any of the unions' suggestions.

65. This ploy was not without precedent. In December 1997, Arafat made the same type of modification to the Palestinian Monetary Authority (PMA) Law, making the PMA governor responsible to the ra'is rather than to the PLC. See "PLC Endorses Monetary Authority Law," *Jerusalem Times,* December 19, 1997.

66. Author interview with Mustafa Barghouthi, Washington, May 12, 1999.

67. Ibid.

68. Interestingly, whereas many legislators were shocked by the August 12 letter, the Palestinian press had recognized the quorum issue and the potential for controversy, immediately after the May 25 PLC vote. See "al-Tashre'i yastakmil al-yawm munaqishat mashru' qanun 'al-b'ia' bil-qira' al-ula" [The PLC Will Complete Discussion of the First Reading of the 'Environment Law' Today], *al-Hayat al-Jadida* online in Arabic, May 27, 1999.

69. Charmaine Seitz, "Seven Days: A Much Awaited Budget Plan," *Palestine Report* 6, vol. 8 (August 18, 1999), an online publication of the Jerusalem Media and Communication Centre.

70. For a lengthy discussion of the problems with the draft law, see PCHR, *Critique of the Party Law 1995 Issued by the Palestinian Authority* (Gaza City: PCHR, 1995).

71. "1995 Draft Political Party Law," Article 4, translation from PCHR, *Critique of the Party Law 1995.*

72. Mashru' Qanun al-Ahzab al-Siyasiyya [Draft Political Parties Law], available in Arabic on the PLC Website.

73. Author interview with Khader el-Moghrabi, February 20, 1999.

74. Author interview with Shaykh Ahmad al-Bahar, February 19, 1999.

75. See PLC Resolution 4/4/378. This particular loan is noteworthy if only to indicate the budding post–Gulf War Palestinian–Kuwaiti rapprochement. The terms of the loan were 3 million Kuwaiti dinars at an interest rate of 3 percent for seventeen years, with a grace period of seven years.

76. PLC Resolution 4/i388/4, June 22, 1999.

77. See "al-Jalsa al-thalitha wa-al-'ashrun lil-Majlis al-Tashre'i" [The Twenty-Third Session of the Legislative Council], *al-Majlis al-Tashre'i Shahriyya,* no. 2 (February 1998), p. 23.

78. This line of questioning may also have intended to point out inconsistencies in Arafat's policies which encourage the growth of

"traditional" familial ties in opposition to more democratic forms of government. A good example of this is Arafat's policy of appointing and supporting family councils in the PA.

79. Erekat repeatedly promised that local elections would be held in Jericho during the summer of 1999. As of December 1999, no local elections had been held. For the PLC position on this issue, see PLC Resolution 3/15/343, December 8, 1998. In this resolution, the PLC resolved that the executive authority should hold elections at the first possible opportunity and before May 4, 1999.

Chapter 5

The PLC and the Peace Process

Since its establishment, the Palestinian Legislative Council (PLC) has on occasion proven to be a complicating factor in the Israeli–Palestinian peace process. In addition to issuing a steady stream of condemnations of Israeli policies ranging from settlements to security, the PLC routinely criticizes the Palestinian Authority (PA) executive for making too many concessions in negotiations. Statements issued by the PLC sometimes even appear to encourage violence against Israelis.

The PLC has been particularly outspoken on the issue of Jerusalem. A statement issued following a special session of the PLC on July 2, 1998, entitled "About the Jerusalem Issue," encapsulates the controversial nature of some of the PLC's peace process–related endeavors.[1] Accusing Israel of "ethnic cleansing" in Jerusalem, the statement calls for the return of eastern Jerusalem to the Palestinians, based on United Nations (UN) Security Council Resolutions 242 and 338. The fate of western Jerusalem, the statement continues, remains under the jurisdiction of UN Resolution 181 and is a matter to be determined during "final status" talks. Several proposals are listed at the end of the statement. One proposal discusses the need for the PLC to pass an unambiguous law declaring Jerusalem as the "eternal capital of the Palestinian people."[2] A second "proposal" cites the need to combat Israeli settlement "by all means," including "armed struggle."[3]

Notwithstanding intermittent incitements to violence, perhaps the most harmful activities of the PLC vis-à-vis the peace process have been a handful of inflammatory legislative initiatives that the PLC has pursued since 1996. Indeed, the PLC has formulated a few extremely provocative laws since it was established. This chapter discusses some of these initiatives, and their potentially adverse affects on the peace process.

Land Law

Qanun tanzim tamlik al-'Ajanib lil-'aqarat fi Falastin, the Law for Regulating Foreign Ownership of Real Estate in Palestine—also known as the Land Law—is probably the most controversial law the PLC has passed since its inception. The draft law was initiated on June 16, 1997, by the PLC Legal Committee, headed by Abdul Karim Abu Saleh—a lawyer and PLC legislator from Khan Yunis, Gaza. It was introduced in the PLC following a few months of high tension between Israelis and Palestinians, which culminated in the renewal of Israeli construction at Har Homa/Jebel Abu Gheneim on the outskirts of Jerusalem.

Palestinian protesters were out in full force when the construction at Har Homa began in May 1997. PA officials strongly opposed the building, and Palestinian protesters engaged in daily scuffles with Israeli police on the perimeter of the construction site. In early May, PA minister of justice Freih Abu Meddien publicly stated that any Palestinian who sold land to Jews would face execution. "Everybody," said Abu Meddien, "now realizes the danger of selling land to a Jew."[4] Abu Meddien's edict was reinforced, and lent a sense of religious legitimacy, when the PA's highest ranking cleric, Mufti Ikrima Sabri, announced later that month:

> Whoever is found to have sold land to Jews, his punishment is death. It is forbidden to pray for him, it is forbidden to purify his body before burial, and it is forbidden to bury him in a Muslim cemetery. We are obligated to remind the public of this religious law, so as not to allow Jews to purchase Arab land and property. . .[5]

From May 4 through June 16, 1997, the PA executed three men without trial for allegedly selling land to Israelis and took dozens more into custody and for interrogation.[6] Vigilantes in the West Bank killed several other suspected land dealers. Based on the timing of the Land Law, it appears that the PLC's goals were twofold. The first priority was to prevent Israelis from making further in-roads to settlement in the West Bank; the second was to lend the face of the rule of law to an official PA policy that encouraged vigilantism and lawlessness.

Within the PLC, the Land Law was highly popular and experienced little opposition in the reading and revision process. In fact, the draft law took less than four months to pass through the PLC's entire legislative process and be referred to PA *ra'is* (president) Yasir Arafat for ratification. The PLC passed the draft land law on September 30 and delivered it to Arafat on October 4, 1997. Given the controversial nature of the law, it is not surprising that as of December 1999—more than two years later—Arafat has neither signed the bill nor allowed it to be published in *al-Jarida al-Rasmiyya* (the *Official Gazette*). The PA law is based on a 1973 Jordanian law called the "Law for Preventing the Sale of Immovable Property to the Enemy," which unambiguously stated that selling land to Jews was punishable by death.[7] In the PA, the sale of land to Jews is considered "high treason." The following excerpted articles from the PLC's Land Law provide a good sense of the legislation:[8]

2 By virtue of the terms of the Law any actions conducted by or being conducted by the occupying authority on Palestinian real estate are considered absolutely null and void. . . .[9]

3 (A) It is prohibited for all persons who are non-Arab Palestinian . . . to possess any real estate in Palestine or to obtain any material right, by any reason of ownership except by inheritance. . . .

3 (C) Occupiers may not be excluded from Article 3 (A). . . .

8 (1) Every Palestinian [who] violates this law has perpetrated the crime of high treason and will be punished according to Criminal Law. . . .

8 (2) Any foreigner who violates the terms of this Law has committed the crime of harming national security and will be punished according to Criminal Law. . . .

10 Anything that contradicts the articles of this Law is nullified. . . .

Immediately after the draft law was publicized in June 1997, Israeli officials voiced their outrage. Israeli government spokesmen termed the law "a violation of the peace accords," and as such, claimed that upon ratification the law could be considered null and void.[10] From a purely technical perspective, Article 2, which purports to invalidate all Israeli laws on "Palestinian real estate," is a *prima facie* contravention of the Israeli–Palestinian Interim Agreement on the West Bank and the Gaza Strip (Oslo II), which obligates the PA to respect the legal rights of Israelis related to land located in the PA.[11] Privately, however, Israeli officials involved with the management of the legal aspects of relations with the PA expressed a more nuanced opposition to the law. While maintaining that the Land Law was in "total contravention" of agreements, Israeli officials confidentially discussed the political ramifications of the precedent of voiding a PLC law *ab initio* (i.e., from the beginning).[12] Israeli officials also privately worried that the law was indeterminate about whether it could be applied retroactively—leaving the door open in the PA for widespread retribution against those who at one time did business with Israelis.

In opposition to the Israelis, the Palestinian leadership was unequivocal in its support for capital punishment. Arafat defended the practice—if not the legal basis for the practice—of executing land dealers. Almost two weeks before the PLC began to debate the law, Arafat condoned the killings that had already taken place. "We are talking," he said, "about a few traitors, and we will apply what has been determined by law against them . . . this is our right and obligation to defend our land."[13] PLC Speaker Abu Ala was another proponent of the death penalty. Unlike Arafat, however, Abu Ala believed that the putative measure should be formalized in law. According to the Speaker, "The current situation makes it necessary that there be strict legislation."[14]

American officials were not so sanguine in their assessment of the PA policy. During the State Department's daily press briefing on May 15, 1997, one month before the PLC began work to codify the death penalty, U.S. State Department spokesman Nicholas Burns said,

> If it turns out that there was any kind of official sanction given to encourage people to go after Arabs who were selling land, then obviously the United States would condemn, in the strongest possible terms, any kind of extrajudicial action that would affect innocent Palestinians. . . . We think it would be good to see a public condemnation of some of these threats by leading Palestinian officials.[15]

PLC Legal Committee chair Abdul Karim Abu Saleh was annoyed with all the controversy surrounding the Land Law. Ignoring the issue of capital punishment, Abu Saleh extolled the law as a practical necessity to "preserve Palestinians' rights."[16] He was also quick to point out that the Jewish National Fund refuses to sell land to Arabs, and that it was once illegal for Palestinian Arabs to own land in Egypt.[17] In the aftermath of the election of Israeli prime minister Ehud Barak, and a week prior to Barak's high-profile visit to Washington to meet with U.S. president Bill Clinton, Abu Saleh revived the issue of the Land Law. He made an impassioned plea for Arafat to ratify the law and vowed to exert pressure via the legislature to have it passed.[18] As of December 1999, the Land Law had progressed no further in the PLC legislative process.

The Firearms and Munitions Law

Under pressure from Israel, the PA developed a law to cover the exigencies related to weapons in PA-controlled territory—including a legal basis for the collection of weapons as mandated by Palestinian–Israeli agreements. In April 1997, the Council of Ministers initiated *Qanun al-'Asliha al-Nariyya wa-al-Thakha'ir*—the Firearms and Munitions Law, also known as the Gun Law—and in May 1998, Arafat ratified the law.

The Gun Law has been widely interpreted as a tool for Palestinians to enforce compliance with their treaty obligations with Israel. Despite ratification in May 1998, the law was not implemented until December 1998—after Israel stipulated, during the Wye River Summit, that further Israeli territorial redeployment would be conditional upon the PA collecting unregistered weapons. In the aftermath of the Wye agreement, on November 19, 1998, Gaza Police chief Ghazi Jabali issued a declaration mandating the implementation of the law beginning December 6.

The Gun Law is divided into five chapters. As is customary, the first chapter provides definitions for the terminology used in the law. The other four chapters concern obtaining and possessing weapons and ammunition; producing, repairing, and importing weapons and ammunition; punishments for violations of the law; and general regulations. For the most part, the law is unexceptional. In Chapter 2, Article 5, the law describes the groups of people prohibited from possessing a weapon, which include anyone under age 21, anyone convicted of a felony or attempted murder, anyone convicted of selling drugs, the mentally handicapped, and anyone who has attempted to commit suicide. Another article discusses licensing procedures and requirements. Notably, the law contains a provision allowing the Ministry of the Interior, which is currently headed by Arafat, to commandeer all privately owned weapons in the West Bank and Gaza in cases of emergency.[19]

Chapters 4 and 5 are relatively straightforward. Chapter 4 discusses punishment guidelines; depending on the nature of the violation, penalties range from a minimum of not more than three months in jail and a fine of 300 Jordanian dinars ($425), to up to three years in prison and a fine of JD5,000 ($7,000). The chapter on general regulations covers a broad range of subjects and, most important, contains the stipulation mandating the surrender of unlicensed weapons to Palestinian authorities.[20]

Israeli officials publicly applauded the post-Wye agreement implementation of the Gun Law, but they privately complain about glaring deficiencies in the law. The deficiencies, they maintain, stem from the fact that the law does not comply with tenets of Israeli–Palestinian agreements. Ironically, the Gun Law—which is such an integral aspect of Israeli–Palestinian security arrangements—may be an Israeli-sanctioned PA violation of Oslo II. Primarily, the controversy and problems with the Gun Law are related to Chapter 3, which deals with the production and importing of weapons and ammunition to the PA.

Chapter 3, Article 17, forbids the production of weapons on Palestinian land except in factories established by, or operated under the supervision of, the PA. Article 19 assigns the power to issue permits to import and export weapons and ammunition to the minister of the interior (i.e., Arafat). Articles 20–22 detail the procedures, prerequisites, and safety precautions required of licensed gun sellers. The final article in the chapter prohibits the shipping of weapons and ammunition either to or from PA territory.

Whereas Chapter 3 may appear to be relatively benign, it is important to note that Oslo II specifically defined the number of automatic weapons permitted to the PA security forces and stipulates, "The Palestinian Police will prevent the manufacture of weapons."[21] Oslo II also specified that the Palestinian police (as opposed to the Ministry of the Interior) would issue licenses allowing possession of handguns in the PA. For several years, Israeli authorities have complained that the PA police force is too large and possesses too many automatic weapons. The Gun Law, according to Israeli officials, is a blatant deviation from the text of Oslo II. One senior Israeli official confided that the Gun Law was "garbage," and sarcastically cited a (fictional) article in the law that "prohibited production or import of cannons into Gaza without a license from the PA."[22]

Because the Gun Law contains clauses mandating the collection of illegal weapons, the Israeli government supported its passage. It appears that, when the Israelis encouraged PA implementation of the Gun Law at Wye Plantation, they were not particularly concerned with the totality of the law and its potential ramifications. As one Israeli said, "We were more concerned with what was happening on the ground than with the laws."[23] In terms of the Gun Law, however, he confided that this strategy did not appear to be working very well. In fact, it was clear by mid-1999 that PA efforts to collect weapons were woefully inadequate. According to Ahmed Sabawi, press officer for the PA preventive security and general intelligence in Gaza, in the preceding twelve months, the PA had confiscated a sum total of only 120 handguns in Gaza.[24] The confiscations did not include assault rifles, rocket-propelled grenade launchers, or any other types of firearms. At the same time, according to Israeli military officials, Palestinians were starting to manufacture submachine guns in Gaza.[25]

National Service Law

Unlike the Gun Law, the draft *Qanun al-Khidma al-Wataniyya* (National Service Law) has not progressed much past infancy. Initiated in August 1997, the law had only reached general discussion by May 1998. Although it has not emerged past its initial reading, the law has already proven controversial. When PLC member Azmi Shuyabi penned the law, he appeared to have the best of intentions; the premise was to mandate one year of "national service" for all Palestinians—men and women—between the ages of 18 and 30. Some of the law's more lofty goals included the "political, economic, and social development of Palestinian society," the encouragement of an "atmosphere of collective work" and "national belonging," and the "protection of the [natural] environment."[26] In addition to these goals, Palestinian legislators believed that mandatory service would decrease unemployment levels and improve morale in Palestinian society. To implement this program, the draft law envisioned the establishment of a bureaucratic and legal framework to process the approximately 30,000–40,000 young Palestinians who would participate in this program annually—and a sizable budget to pay for it all.

Critics were quick to point out a few vague articles in the draft law that gave the impression that it would constitute the beginning of Palestinian military conscription. Foremost among these was Article 11, which discussed how the goals of the law would be accomplished by "assisting in the protection of institutions and public facilities in the cities and villages and governorates in coordination with determined authorities."[27] Indeed, Shuyabi himself confirmed the general suspicion that the national service law would be used as a conscription mechanism; he repeatedly volunteered that the law would eventually be "amended to include a proposal for weapons training" so that the youth could adequately defend national institutions.[28] Some PLC members, like Interior and Security Committee chair Fakhri Shakoura, were incensed that the draft law did not *already* contain provisions for military training. In reporting his committee's comments on the draft law, Shakoura said that, insofar as it did not specifically include clauses mandating military training and preparation, the law was a "national laughingstock and not a national service."[29]

Shuyabi realized that both the draft law and his accompanying statements would be particularly controversial; after all, Oslo II specified a numerical limit for Palestinian policemen in the PA and unambiguously outlawed Palestinian conscription. Still, Shuyabi maintained that, whereas weapons training might be against the "spirit" of Oslo, it was not against the "letter" of the agreement.[30] Predictably, the Israelis were infuriated with the national service law. David Bar-Illan, then the communications director for Prime Minister Binyamin Netanyahu, called the law a "camouflage for openly setting up an army draft," and a "severe violation of the Oslo accords."[31]

As it does with many other laws, the PLC's Parliamentary Research Unit (PRU) produced a short, internal document analyzing the draft law. This document, titled *Mulahathat hawl mashru' qanun al-khidma al-Wataniyya* (Remarks on the National Service Law), discussed some of the practical problems that would be encountered during the law's implementation.[32] These included the fact that Palestinian women who are 30 years old would already have "five or six children," and it would be impractical for these women to leave home to live in barracks. The document also raised the question of funding, inquiring whether it would be appropriate to have such a program funded by international donors.

In addition to these practical questions, the report highlighted perhaps the most salient topic brought to the fore by the draft law: Why would the PA need this law? In response, the PRU document explored two opinions. One explanation was that the law was necessary because it related to the question of Palestinian nation building and integration of people into a future Palestinian state. The second opinion cited in the PRU report indicated that the law—complete with its military and security aspects—was relevant because of the future "likely confrontation" with Israel. Interestingly, the PRU report noted that the law was problematic on two fronts. First, the law was in direct conflict with Israeli–Palestinian peace agreements. And second, the PRU was concerned with the establishment of yet another security apparatus and bureaucracy, as well as with the interaction between this new apparatus and the already numerous extant security apparati.

Miscellaneous Activities

Provocative PLC activities, and other PLC activities related to peace process issues, have not focused solely on legislative efforts. In October 1997, for example, PLC members sought to punish Israel for not honoring its agreements by issuing a resolution requesting the executive authority to boycott the Doha economic summit.[33] Likewise, following the mysterious death of Hamas military leader Mohi al-Din al-Sharif in 1998, the legislature established a committee to investigate the demise of the "martyred struggler." In September 1998, the PLC resolved to issue a press release condemning American "aggression" following a U.S. cruise missile attack against suspected Usama bin Laden targets in Afghanistan and Sudan.

One of the more controversial issues on the PLC agenda has been the issue of PA security detainees. Since its establishment, the PLC has been an outspoken advocate for Hamas "political" prisoners detained in PA jails.[34] In early January 1999, alarmed by what was described as a lack of due process afforded to approximately three hundred Hamas members—many of whom had been imprisoned without charge since the run-up to the March 1996 Sharm al-Shaykh antiterrorism summit—the PLC discussed the legality of this executive authority practice. This issue generated so much support and enthusiasm among legislators that the PLC convened in special session on January 13, 1999, and threatened to vote no confidence in Arafat's administration if the prisoners were not either released or tried by the Muslim holiday 'Eid al-Fitr, which was to begin January 18.[35]

On January 17, 1999, PA officials announced that "a number" of Hamas prisoners had been released, and said several more would be released the following day in celebration of the holiday.[36] According to the PA, ninety "Islamic activists" were released for 'Eid al-Fitr.[37] Not impressed, PLC members dismissed those freed as being regular criminals, not Hamas members.[38] Although some further meetings were held on this issue, no vote of no confidence resulted.

The issue of "political" prisoners is one of the few topics on which the PLC consistently confronts Arafat. Interestingly, while Fatah is generally a stalwart of support for the ra'is, when it comes to Hamas prisoners in PA jails, Arafat cannot maintain party discipline in the legislature. PLC members sympathize with the Islamist prisoners and are extremely critical of Arafat for pursuing a policy that appears to be an unwarranted and humiliating concession to Israel. Support for Hamas prisoners is good political publicity in the PA and clearly strikes a personal chord with many of the legislators.

In addition to being highly critical of the PA policy on "political" prisoners, the PLC has been a strong proponent for the release of Palestinian prisoners—Islamist or otherwise—in Israeli jails. PLC Resolution 3/16/350, issued on December 21, 1998, for example, demanded that the executive authority and the Palestinian negotiating team begin to view the issue of prisoners in Israeli jails as "a priority."

Jerusalem—a particularly charged peace process issue—has also been a topic of primary concern for the PLC and a staple on the agenda since the PLC's establishment. Since 1997, the PLC has issued several resolutions about Jerusalem, condemning Israeli policies and encouraging a more activist Palestinian policy in the city. In 1999, for example, a PLC resolution encouraged the PA to purchase schools and property in Jerusalem.[39] This type of behavior was exhibited by a March 1999 PLC resolution that requested that Minister of Planning and International Cooperation Nabil Sha'ath and Jerusalem member Hatem Abdul Qader write a letter to the

European Union (EU) on behalf of the PLC regarding the EU position on final status issues. This PLC focus on Jerusalem has strayed into the realm of international relations and final-status issues—which the terms of Oslo II characterize as "off limits."

The PLC and Peace

Despite Israeli–Palestinian agreements, the PLC consistently engages in prohibited activities. These undertakings, many of which concern permanent status and other security-related issues, have been adopted as permanent elements of PLC legislative and oversight responsibilities. The composition of the twelve PLC standing committees is perhaps the best proof of how ingrained these activities are. Two if not three of these committees—the Jerusalem Committee, the (Israeli) Settlements Committee, and perhaps the Refugee Committee—are technically not compliant with Palestinian commitments to Israel. Yet these committees were constituted in 1996, only months after the legislature was established.

Israel understandably considers many of the PLC's peace process–related endeavors to be provocative—but it recognizes that they are not particularly important in terms of having a real effect on the ground. In this regard, the land law drafted by the PLC is instructive. Although considered offensive, the draft law basically only codified the already existing policy in the PA. To Israel, these initiatives are largely perceived as annoyances, more symbolic than effective.

Of course, a convincing argument could be made that, if the PLC suddenly gained more power, its ongoing activities that complicate the peace process would take on greater significance. This might be the case were the power to be gained in the short run. In the long term, however, it is unlikely that the PLC would constitute a peace process irritant. Two factors in particular would mitigate in favor of a more moderate PLC: the regional trend toward less "ideological" and more pragmatic governments, and the fact that an empowered PLC would be a more integral part of the PA—and would, over time, be coopted into the PA system. (In addition to these factors, it should be noted that it is unlikely that the PLC will gain a significant amount of power in the very near future.)

The relative position of the PLC vis-à-vis the executive has encouraged a radicalism in the legislature. In a sense, the legislature can afford to be provocative precisely because it has no power. But if the PLC attained decision-making authority, so the logic goes, its positions would start to matter, and its new circumstances would compel a shift toward moderation. The same would likely be true if Islamist candidates—from either Hamas or *Hizb al-Khalas* (the Redemption Party)—were to win seats in the next PLC elections. Studies indicate that, once they enter parliament, Islamists and other factions with militant platforms tend to behave more responsibly.[40] More power does not necessarily imply more irresponsibility. For the PLC, an increased amount of authority and influence in the political system will necessitate the adoption of a more moderate, pragmatic approach.

Notes

1. "Hawl qadaya al-Quds" [About the Jerusalem Issue], *al-Majlis al-Tashre'i Shahriyya Natiqa bi-ism al- Majlis al-Tashre'i al-Falastini* [Palestinian Legislative Council Monthly], no. 5 (1998), pp. 48–49.

2. Ibid.; see especially Proposal 4.

3. Ibid.; see especially Proposal 10.

4. Joel Greenberg, "Arab's Death and the Selling of Land to Jews," *New York Times*, May 12, 1997, p. 3.

5. Christopher Walker, "Arafat Threatens to Execute Arabs Who Sell Land to Jews," *Times* (London), May 22, 1997. See also *Yediot Ahronot*, May 20, 1997.

6. "Arafat Says He Would Arrest Killers of Land Dealers," Reuters, June 8, 1997.

7. See Article 4 of the Jordanian "Law for Preventing the Sale of Immovable Property to the Enemy," which appeared in Alexander Safian, "Can Arabs Buy Land in Israel?" *Middle East Quarterly* (December 1997), p. 15.

8. English translation from the official PLC Website at http://www.pal-plc.org. The Arabic original is also available on the Website.

9. The law defines the *occupying authority* and *occupiers* as "the occupying Israeli government and its civil and military institutions, its imperialist colonizers, the settlers, and those under [the government's] control."

10. "PA Legislators Debate New, Radical Land Sales Law," Agence France Presse, June 16, 1997, in Foreign Broadcast Information Service (FBIS)–Near East and South Asia (FBIS-NES-97-167), June 17, 1997.

11. See *Israeli–Palestinian Interim Agreement on the West Bank and Gaza Strip,* September 28, 1995, available online from the Israeli Ministry of Foreign Affairs Website, http://www.mfa.gov.il. Specifically, see Chapter 2: Redeployment and Security Arrangements, Article 20(3); and Annex III: Protocol Concerning Civil Affairs, Article 22(3), on land registration.

12. Israeli officials also pointed out that the draft law used the wording "Palestine" in both headings and in the body of the text. This usage, they maintained, raised questions as to the "good faith" of the PA.

13. "Arafat Defends Execution of Arab Sellers of Land to Jews," Agence France Presse, May 21, 1997.

14. Samar Assad, "Arafat Government Sets Price for Land Sales: Death," *Washington Times,* May 6, 1997.

15. U.S. Department of State, Daily Press Briefing, May 15, 1997, online at http://secretary.state.gov.

16. Author interview with Abdul Karim Abu Saleh, February 17, 1999.

17. Abu Saleh's claims about the Jewish National Fund (JNF) are inaccurate. In fact, the JNF does not "sell" land to either Arabs or Jews; it leases land to both Jewish and Arab Israelis. For a detailed discussion of this issue, see Safian, "Can Arabs Buy Land in Israel?"

18. Tahsin al-Istal, "Abu Saleh: Qanun tanzim tamlik al-'ajanib lil-'aqarat yuhmi maqdirat sh'bana" [Abu Saleh: The Law for Foreign Ownership of Real Estate Protects the Abilities of Our People], *al-Hayat al-Jadida,* July 8, 1999, online in Arabic at http://www.alhayat-j.com.

19. *Qanun al-'Asliha al-Nariyya wa-al-Thakha'ir* [Gun Law], Chapter 2, Article 12, May 20, 1998, available on the PLC Website.

20. See Chapter 5, Article 27 of the Gun Law.

21. See *Israeli–Palestinian Interim Agreement on the West Bank and the Gaza Strip,* September 28, 1995. For the number of automatic weapons

permitted to the security forces, see Annex I, article IV (5). In the West Bank, this included up to 4,000 rifles, up to 4,000 pistols and up to 120 machine guns. In Gaza, Palestinian police were permitted up to 7,000 light personal weapons and up to 120 machine guns. Concerning the manufacture of weapons, see Annex I, article XI (2) (f).

22. Author interview with IDF official in Tel Aviv, February 21, 1998. Israelis are particularly concerned with the amount of weapons possessed by the Palestinian civilian population.

23. Ibid.

24. "IMRA Interviews Press Officer of PA Preventive Security," *Independent Media Review and Analysis* (IMRA), July 8, 1999.

25. Israeli sources in the Defense Ministry indicate that the Palestinians operate several small factories and workshops that produce automatic weapons.

26. See *Qanun al-Khidma al-Wataniyya* (National Service Law), Article 10, May 1998, available in Arabic on the PLC Website.

27. Ibid., Article 11, clause 7.

28. Jon Immanuel, "PA: We're Protecting Officials Against Israeli Attacks," *Jerusalem Post*, August 24, 1997.

29. See "al-Jalsa al-sabia'a: al-dawra al-thalitha" [The Seventh Session: the Third Round], *al-Majlis al-Tashre'i Shahriyya*, no. 5 (1998), p. 24.

30. Immanuel, "PA: We're Protecting Officials."

31. Ibid.

32. *Mulahathat hawl mashru' al-qanun al-khidma al-wataniyya* [Remarks on the National Service Law], no. 98-22 (al-Bireh: Parliamentary Research Unit, 1998).

33. PLC Resolution 2/21/211, passed October 27–29, 1997. The resolution accused Israel of "disavowing" and refusing to implement its agreements with the Palestine Liberation Organization (PLO).

34. Islamist "political" prisoners are not to be confused with the "security" prisoners currently held without charge by the PA. "Security" prisoners include suspected collaborators with Israel and are allegedly held by the Military Intelligence units of the PA police forces. For more details on this, see Amnesty International, "PA Defying the Rule of Law: Political Detainees Held without Charge or Trial," AI Index MDE 21/03/99, April 1999.

35. Jamila Sydam, a female legislator from Deir-al-Balah, Gaza, was a leading proponent for the vote of no confidence. For further details, see "I'lan 'an tashkil lajna khasa li-mutaba'at mawdu' al-'ifraj 'an al-mu'taqlin" [The Announcement of the Formation of a Special Committee Tasked with the Issue of Releasing the Prisoners], *al-Hayat al-Jadida*, January 14, 1999, online in Arabic. See also PLC Resolution 3/I10/359, January 13, 1999.

36. Imad al-Franji, "al-Sulta al-Wataniyya tafraj 'an sujana' wa-mu'taqalin bi-munasabat al-'Eid" [The PA Releases Imprisoned and Detained on the Occasion of the Eid], *al-Quds*, January 18, 1999, online in Arabic at http://www.alquds.com.

37. "PLC Begins Discussion on Political Prisoners in Ramallah," Middle East News Line, January 27, 1999.

38. The Prime Minister's Office in Israel maintained that among those released were five killers of U.S. citizens. See "Israel Prime Minister's Office Press Release," January 28, 1999, via "Arafat Releases Five Killers of Americans," IMRA, January 29, 1999.

39. PLC Resolution 4/5/381, May 25, 1999.

40. For a more complete discussion of this issue, see Abdo Baaklini, Guilain Denoeux, and Robert Springborg, *Legislative Politics in the Arab World* (Boulder, Colo.: Lynne Rienner, 1999).

Chapter 6

Israel, the United States, and the PLC

In the previous chapters, this study described the structure, role, and activities of the Palestinian Legislative Council (PLC), as well as the hostile milieu in which the legislature operates. Since its establishment, the PLC has been subjected to a continuous onslaught by the executive. At this point, it is unclear what the long-term effects of these initial experiences will be for Palestinian governance.

But if the implications of the PLC's initial setbacks are significant for Palestinians, they are also considerable for Israel and the United States. This chapter addresses the policies of Israel and the United States regarding the nature of Palestinian governance and the connection between governance and the potential for a sustainable peace in the region.

Israel and the PLC

In the Israeli government, the PLC inspires ambivalence.[1] Many Israeli officials say they would prefer a democratic—rather than authoritarian—Palestinian Authority (PA) neighbor, and hence would support a stronger PLC. Not surprisingly, though, most Israelis value security more than they value democracy. Privately, many Israelis acknowledge that there is no contradiction between security and democracy, and they admit that a strong legislature would probably not decrease the ability of PA *ra'is* (president) Yasir Arafat to continue to control the security situation in the PA. At the same time, however, Israeli officials appear to be more comfortable with Arafat than with the unknown—and presumably unpredictable—PLC. It is assumed that any power gain for the PLC will be at the expense of Arafat, whom the Israelis consider to be the best Palestinian guarantor of their security. As long as Arafat provides the requisite security, Israel will remain neutral on the issue of Palestinian governance.

Israeli officials in the Foreign Ministry admit that, whereas the structure of the government in the PA is "more or less" what was discussed in the Oslo accords, the power relations between the executive authority and the PLC have been inverted in such a way that inhibits democratic development. Interestingly, although the 1995 Israeli–Palestinian Interim Agreement on the West Bank and the Gaza Strip—Oslo II—established a democratic framework for the PA, it could not mandate democracy. In fact, the agreement contains elements that could encourage and sustain either democracy or autocracy. This contradictory situation seems to reflect the desires of the individuals involved in constructing the agreement. Arafat sought a strong executive to maintain his preeminent position. Israeli prime minister Yitzhak Rabin also preferred a strong Arafat who would not be hampered by democratic staples—such as human rights and due process—in his promised fight against Palestinian Islamic militants. Other Israelis and Palestinians involved with the Oslo process took a longer-term view that a democratic PA would be more conducive to a lasting peace, but apparently these views did not prevail.[2]

In terms of specific concerns, the Legal Department at the Israeli Foreign Ministry, the Legal Assistance Division of the Ministry of Justice, and the International Law Department in the Israel Defense Forces, have been focused primarily on what they consider to be serious, or "insufferable," violations of the agreements by the PLC. Israeli concerns with the PLC generally fit into two categories: symbolic actions and legislative initiatives. In terms of the PLC's symbolic actions, Israeli officials cite as "bothersome infractions" the various PLC activities in the field of international relations and attempts by the legislative body to sign international agreements and obtain membership in international organizations. These infractions also include PLC activities in Jerusalem. The Israeli prime minister's Website, for example, points out that "many of the seven Jerusalem representatives on the PLC operated out of offices located in Jerusalem"—in "violation" of the Oslo accords.[3]

More troublesome to Israeli officials, though, are some legislative endeavors that the Israelis consider to be incompatible with existing agreements. One Foreign Ministry official mentioned the PLC's draft "water" legislation—which presupposes the existence of a Palestinian state and touches on issues that by agreement should be relegated to "final status" talks—as an example of this type of infraction. The draft water law under discussion is a particularly controversial piece of legislation because it deals with issues of sovereignty and regulation of water resources, including but not limited to navigation in the Sea of Galilee (Lake Kinneret), the Jordan River, and aquifers. Other examples of this type of legislation are the draft land law, the draft national service law, and the ratified Civil Defense Law.[4] Likewise, Israeli officials often complain that, in contravention of Oslo II, the PLC does not "notify" Israeli authorities of pending legislation. Rather, the Palestinians merely inform their Israeli counterparts when a bill has passed; the Israelis are effectively delivered *faits accomplis.*

Despite these annoyances, Israeli officials do not appear to be particularly concerned with the nature of Palestinian governance. If anything, there appears to be a tendency to give the inexperienced PA the benefit of the doubt. Pointing out that Israel, too, had antidemocratic tendencies in its first two decades, one senior official in the Israeli Ministry of Foreign Affairs urged patience. He said, "Following the final-status agreement, hopefully there will be a more democratic administration."

For Israel, the issue of the PLC is closely tied to the matter of succession in the PA. Under Arafat, there is little hope that the PLC will take on a more prominent role. The real question for Israel is what role the PLC will play after Arafat. Israeli officials recognize the potential, under different circumstances, for the PLC to play a dramatically different role in the PA. According to Joel Singer, the Israeli lawyer who served as a primary author of the Oslo accords,

> The framers of the Interim Agreement provided a blueprint for a democratic Palestinian system of self-government; its full implementation is now in the hands of the Palestinians of the West Bank and the Gaza Strip. Only they can decide whether they want to develop the type of democracy that provides a truly representative government which fully protects all the rights of all its residents.[5]

Essentially, by placing the onus of good governance on the Palestinians themselves, Singer exempts Israel from playing a role in the shaping the future of PA governance. There is some logic to his position. After all, Israeli initiatives within the PA are typically viewed by Palestinians with suspicion. Nevertheless, it is in Israel's long-term interest to have a democratic Palestinian neighbor. Therefore, subtly but surely, the Israeli government should attempt to encourage better governance in the PA. At the very least, Israel can support democratic institutions in the PA by establishing and maintaining formalized and regularly scheduled visits and exchanges between the Knesset and the PLC.

U.S. Policy and the PLC

> *"Experience has shown that democracies are the best partners for making peace and building prosperity."*
>
> —Robert Pelletreau, assistant secretary of state for Near Eastern affairs[6]

In January 1996, Robert Pelletreau applauded what would be the first-ever elections in the PA. Pelletreau characterized the elections as a first step toward democracy and an important "part of the process to validate [Israeli–Palestinian] agreements." Whereas Pelletreau's linkage between democracy and peace may seem intuitive, it stands out as one of the most straightforward and unambiguous U.S. policy pronouncements in support of democracy in the PA. In fact, however, it is far from clear that the United States supports Palestinian democracy. When asked in June 1996 whether democracy was a prerequisite for peace in the Middle East, Martin Indyk presented an altogether different perspective. Indyk, the U.S. ambassador to Israel, said, "We [the United States] accept Arab countries as they are."[7]

To be sure, U.S. officials have given some verbal encouragement to democratization in the PA, but not as much as one would expect. In July 1994, shortly before Arafat's arrival in Gaza, then–Secretary of State Warren Christopher challenged the Palestinians to "govern wisely and well."[8] In May 1995, President Bill Clinton discussed the importance of establishing the rule of law in the PA. "The peace," he said, "will never succeed" without this.[9] Likewise, prior to the Palestinian elections in 1996, State Department spokesman Nicholas Burns mentioned America's "long-term objective of helping to build democracy and rule of law" in the PA.[10] More recently, on September 12, 1997, Secretary of State Madeleine Albright made a radio address to the PA, during which she acknowledged Palestinian democratic aspirations and lent the U.S. imprimatur to the undertaking. Albright said, "You [Palestinians] have shown a clear desire to establish a thriving and democratic Palestinian society. In that effort, America wants you to succeed."[11]

The most consistent U.S. message of support for democratization in the PA, however, came from the chief U.S. diplomatic contact with the PA, then–Consul General in Jerusalem Edward Abington. In 1997, Abington made a particularly impassioned plea for Palestinian democracy and a strong Palestinian legislature. "The United States," he said, "strongly supports the establishment of strong Palestinian democratic institutions . . . and one of the most critical institutions is the Palestinian Legislative Council."[12] Abington's advocacy on behalf of the PLC did not waver, even though he recognized that, in terms of the peace process, democracies "complicate things."[13] Despite the explicit nature of these remarks, the fact remains that Abington—who was then working as a diplomat in the field—was allowed to be the sole purveyor of this policy, without any consistent backup from his colleagues in Washington. The absence of this message in Washington sends a signal, deliberate or otherwise, as to the priority of the policy.

Although there is little doubt that Washington—at least in theory—would welcome a more representative, pluralistic, and democratic system of government in the PA, there is some question as to the extent to which the United States will go to encourage this development. Statements by high-ranking U.S. officials notwithstanding, the administration has offered little substantive encouragement for democratization in the PA. Whereas Washington provides financial support for projects promoting good governance in the PA, it does not forcefully persuade Arafat to implement the rule of law.

In December 1998, President Clinton paid a historic visit to Gaza to witness a special session of Palestinian leaders confirm the amendment of the PLO's charter. In his speech to the assembled gathering, during which the President touched on subjects ranging from the peace process and economic development to health care and water, one theme was conspicuously absent: democracy. Indeed, the word itself was only mentioned once during the trip, in a brief reference to U.S. foreign assistance to the PA.[14] For the time being, it appears that Palestinian democratic development has been placed on the back burner of U.S. policy priorities.

Apparent inconsistencies in U.S. policy toward the PA may be related to a longstanding Washington debate that pits the benefits of democracy against the benefits of stability, security, and peace. To be sure, the political and strategic dividends of autocratic governments in the Middle East are well documented. Despite public opinion, for example, Egypt and Jordan were able to forge ahead with and enforce unpopular peace treaties with Israel. The Egyptian and Jordanian precedents are proof that strong governments with the veneer but not the substance of democracy, can—at least in the short run—deliver peace and stability. Is this the type of arrangement that the United States has in mind for the PA?

Since 1994, when Arafat returned triumphally to Gaza, the U.S. government has sidestepped questions regarding the undemocratic nature of the PA. Instead, Washington has preferred to emphasize the outstanding performance of the PA—and Ra'is Arafat in particular—on the peace-process front.[15] Because it is believed that Arafat can "deliver" Palestinian support for a final status agreement with Israel, Washington has paid little attention to the prevalent human rights abuses and the systematic disregard for democratic processes in the PA.[16] To this end, Washington has been very careful not to embarrass Arafat publicly or do anything that might strengthen his adversaries. The mild U.S. initiative in 1997 encouraging Arafat to sign *al-Qanun al-'Asasi* (the Basic Law) constituted an anomaly in U.S. policy that has not since been repeated. The extent to which the administration has endeavored to coddle the PA is remarkable. In June 1999, for example, Martin Indyk cited the PA as a successful example of Middle Eastern "political liberalization." Not only were women voting in Qatar, he said—the PA was "being held to account by an elected Palestinian Legislative Council."[17] Despite this positive appraisal of the efficacy of the PLC, since 1996, the will of the Palestinian legislature has consistently been frustrated by an obstructionist executive.

U.S. support for Arafat may, in some part, be based on a perceived lack of choices. Arafat has been so dominant a figure in the PLO that he has eclipsed other potential Palestinian leaders. Now a septuagenarian and reportedly in ill health, the question of Arafat's succession has taken on a new sense of urgency. Among Palestinians, and in wider Arab public opinion, there is a consensus that the United States has a clear preference for a Palestinian "strongman" successor. It is widely rumored, for example, that U.S. policymakers consider Jibril Rajoub, head of the Preventive Security Force (PSF) in the West Bank, and Muhammad Dahlan, head of the PSF in Gaza, to be the preferred successors to Arafat. Some reports have even indicated that Washington has been actively promoting Rajoub among U.S. allies in the region.[18] That such views are widely held reflects a common belief among Palestinians—and Arabs in general—that the West prefers continuity and fears that a different form of government in the PA might not be as sympathetic toward the peace process.

If so, the U.S. policy vis-à-vis the PLC and Palestinian governance is myopic. Unlike Jordan and Egypt, the nature of an

Israeli–Palestinian peace agreement will require popular consensus. Egypt and Jordan were not required to make significant concessions in their peace agreements with Israel. It is all but certain, however, that in any deal with the Israelis, the Palestinians will be compelled to accept territorial compromise. This fundamental difference between the Egyptian and Jordanian cases and the Palestinian one will necessitate the development of a Palestinian government that is more democratic.

In 1995, almost one year after the PA was established, Lisa Anderson, a political scientist at Columbia University, observed, "For the moment, peace and democracy appear to be mutually exclusive for the Palestinians."[19] At the start of a new century, the Palestinian government is still more authoritarian than democratic. Yet, the PA appears to have reached a crossroads of sorts. On the verge of attaining statehood, and integrally involved in the peace process, Palestinians are finding their way between democracy and dictatorship. The coming years will likely set the precedent for the future of Palestinian governance. Washington has political currency and credibility among Palestinians, and hence can play an important role in determining the future character of the PA. Thus far, the United States has proven unwavering in its support for Arafat. Despite this, however, Washington is keeping one foot in the "democracy" door and providing some financial support to the Palestinian Legislative Council.

U.S. Development Projects and the PLC

Efforts by the U.S. Agency for International Development (USAID) to promote democratization in the West Bank and Gaza began in earnest in 1994, with the provision of more than $2 million in funding to support preparations for the 1996 Palestinian elections. From 1993 to 1998, USAID democratization obligations in the Palestinian Authority (PA) reached nearly $36 million, or about 10 percent of the $375 million allocated to USAID's West Bank and Gaza programs.[20] More recently, though, USAID has begun to recognize democratization in the PA as a higher priority. The agency's congressional requests for democratization funding hovered at about $10 million annually for fiscal years 1998 and 1999. For 2000, however, USAID requested $17 million from Congress to establish "more responsive and accountable governance" in the PA.[21]

Since 1996, a linchpin in USAID's strategic objective of "democracy and governance" has been the provision of support to the PLC. Accordingly, significant financial resources were devoted to strengthening the capacity of the legislature from 1996 through 1999.[22] In coordination with European donors, USAID has administered a few large technical assistance projects working with the PLC, spending roughly $6 million on the nascent institution. Although detailed breakdowns of expenditures are difficult to obtain, the lion's share of USAID funding for the PLC was divided between the International Republican Institute (IRI) and Associates for Rural Development (ARD).[23]

In addition to U.S. contractors, USAID has also implemented some projects via Palestinian nongovernmental organizations (NGOs). These NGOs have received—and continue to receive—grant funding from USAID to work on the strategic objective of democratization. In 1997, for example, USAID granted a total of $1.1 million to four Palestinian NGOs involved with civil society projects.[24] The grants given to Palestinian NGOs in 1997 constituted about 23 percent of

Total Democracy and Governance Obligations

Fiscal Year	**Obligations in 000's**	**of which to U.S. NGOs**	**of which to Pal. NGOs**
1994/1995:	$5,974	$5,455	$0
1996:	$9,500	$6,518	$0
1997:	$9,834	$3,200	$1,007
1998:	$10,721	$2,927	$4,600

Total obligated to assist the PLC for fiscal years 1994–1998: $7,864.

Note: The official data from the USAID mission in Tel Aviv aggregates fiscal years 1994 and 1995.
Source: Democracy and Governance Section, USAID, Washington.

the total USAID funding for the development of civil society. In contrast, USAID has provided no direct funding to Palestinian NGOs working with the PLC; these groups are funded through subcontracts with U.S. contractors.

In September 1996, Vermont-based ARD began working on a three-year, $4-million contract to provide technical assistance to the PLC in drafting legislation, lending oversight to the executive authority, improving legislative efficiency, streamlining administrative processes, and encouraging legislative outreach. At about the same time, a USAID grant funded the IRI to begin working in collaboration with a Nablus-based NGO, the Center for Palestine Research and Studies (CPRS), to establish the Parliamentary Research Unit (PRU).[25] Modeled on the Congressional Research Service, the PRU was established to provide Palestinian legislators with an in-house source of objective research and information to facilitate and better inform the decision-making process.[26]

Operating from a large office in the basement of the PLC office in al-Bireh, the PRU appears to be exercising its role as an independent source of information and data for legislators. By way of fulfilling its mission, the PRU issues analyses and critiques of PLC laws, pointing out inconsistencies and potential problems with draft legislation. In 1997 and 1998 for example, the PRU published several internal documents en route to the PLC's passage of the judiciary law, including an eight page, detailed review of the bill and a lengthy and detailed comparison of judicial independence in the PA, Jordan, Egypt, and Israel.[27] In October 1999, the PRU staff was working on a critical analysis of a draft law regulating the Palestinian stock market. The main consumers of PRU information are the PLC standing committees. Each of these twelve committees has at least one employee seconded from the PRU to take care of the everyday research and policy analysis needs of the committee.

Although the PRU may eventually establish itself as an integral element of the legislative process, most legislators currently do not take full advantage of its services. Some Palestinians familiar with the PRU whisper that the organization is ill-equipped to respond to many complex technical requests. At times, to compensate for an absence of in-house expertise, the PRU is compelled to bring in outside experts and consultants. In 1996–97, for example, ARD subcontracted a local affiliate of Arthur Andersen to provide technical assistance for budget analysis. The PRU's weakness appears to lie primarily in providing advice on technically complex issues, like economics and healthcare.

To remedy this situation, in the near future USAID will likely subcontract the Ramallah-based *Ma'had 'Abhath al-Siyasat al-Iqtisadiyya al-Falastini* (Palestine Economic Policy Research Institute, better known by its Arabic acronym, MAS) to train Budget Committee and PRU staffers in budget analysis techniques. In 1998, ARD brought in outside experts to assist with the drafting of the judiciary law. ARD has also engaged outside expertise to assist the PLC to draft a tax law, labor law, banking law, and securities law. It appears that USAID is starting to take some interest in improving the quality of the legislation emanating from the PLC. A 1999 USAID request for funding proposals specified that the "contractor will work with the Council in developing mechanisms for increasing its access to information and expertise in the legislative review process."[28]

ARD has the largest USAID-funded project working with the PLC. Since 1996, ARD has provided technical support to the legislature in three crucial areas: oversight and monitoring of the executive authority; drafting and reviewing legislation; and strengthening constituent relations. ARD's three-year contract ended in September 1999. Palestinian legislators, PLC staffers, and USAID, by and large, were pleased with ARD's work on the ground, and in early September, ARD won the USAID rebid on the PLC support contract. The new PLC project is a three-year, $8-million contract—double the size of ARD's previous PLC project. Along with an expanded scope of work, the increased allocation of aid dollars to the PLC is indicative of the fact that the U.S. government is starting to consider the PLC a crucial element for the future of Palestinian governance.[29] USAID's program goals for the PLC from 1999 through 2002 were formalized on October 14, 1999, when top USAID officials visited Ramallah to sign a Memorandum of Understanding (MOU). One explicit priority of the new MOU is the development of relations between the executive authority and the PLC. The MOU was signed by Ahmed Qurie (Abu Ala), the PLC Speaker, and Larry Garber, USAID's West Bank/Gaza mission director. (See Appendix VI.)

Although the PLC has a long way to go in terms of asserting its authority and assuming its appropriate role vis-à-vis the executive authority, the PLC has demonstrated both an anecdotal and empirical improvement in its performance. USAID technical assistance, and ARD's project in particular, may in some part be responsible for the improvement. Statistics gathered by ARD to fulfill USAID reporting requirements indicate an increased level in PLC activity from 1996 through 1998. In 1997, for example, the PLC passed six laws; in 1998, it passed fourteen.[30] Likewise, during each year from 1996 through 1998, the PLC exhibited an increase in the number of oversight proceedings it initiated on executive authority actions. ARD also documented improvements in members' constituent relations and a more active role for committees in the legislative process.

In addition to training legislators and committee staffers, in 1998, as part of a separate USAID contract, ARD installed and implemented a Hansard verbatim transcript system in the PLC and equipment to record the floor votes of PLC members. Verbatim transcripts are now made of all PLC plenary sessions. Within the next year, if Abu Ala agrees to the project, the PLC may start to issue transcripts of legislative proceedings to the press or make them available online. Currently, although the equipment is installed, PLC members' votes are taken by a counting of hands—vote tallies are not recorded and are not typically published in the press. When voting records become more widely available, members of the legislature may start to feel more accountable to their constituents.

Palestinian awareness of the PLC is also bound to increase when television coverage of the legislature—which has been absent since Palestinian journalist Daoud Kuttab was arrested in 1997—once again returns to the PA airwaves. In 1997, USAID provided *al-Quds TV* with a $25,000 pilot grant to cover start-up costs for Kuttab's now-defunct parliamentary broadcasts. A forthcoming USAID project will sponsor technical assistance to the Palestinians so they can start broadcasting live sessions of the PLC, along the lines of C-SPAN.

The PLC and the Peace Process

In Israel and the United States there has been a stunning silence about the lack of democratic development in the PA. With pressing concerns like security and peace-process progress, luxuries like good governance get little attention. Within this environment, PLC efforts to promote a more accountable Palestinian government have not fared well. At the same time, however, PLC endeavors that have constituted a problem for the peace process have been well publicized. The relatively few initiatives of the PLC that have been counterproductive to the peace process have largely overshadowed the important and productive work of the elected body.

Although certain U.S. officials quietly admit that they find Arafat's disposition toward the PLC to be distressing, conventional Washington wisdom supports a continuation of the status quo in the PA. It is troubling that Arafat has consistently obstructed the legislative and monitoring roles of the PLC. But Arafat's antidemocratic behavior has, at times, also thwarted what would have been legislative violations of Palestinian agreements with Israel. This is perhaps best exemplified by Arafat's refusal since 1997 to ratify the land law; it is likewise conceivable that if and when it is passed by the PLC, Arafat might oppose legislative will on the national service law. Similarly, despite strong PLC pressure, Arafat has thus far kept many top Hamas security risk individuals in PA prisons. Given that "democratic" institutions in the PA have at times undermined peace-process goals, a legitimate argument could be made that Arafat's authoritarian system of rule might in fact be better for the peace process in the short term.

Still, despite occasionally provocative initiatives, resolutions, and legislation, it is not clear that the PLC is any more problematic than is Arafat when it comes to advancing the peace process. Authoritarian government in the PA has some short-term benefits for the peace process, but it may prove more problematic in the long run. Arafat's insistence on exercising his own personal discretion on all significant financial matters—which is reflected by the PLC's problems in passing annual budget laws—almost assures the continued financial straits of the PA. Lack of economic development appears to be a major impediment to progress on the peace process. Likewise, the executive authority's reluctance to have local council elections—despite the 1996 PLC law mandating them to do so—puts democracy on indefinite hold in the PA. Many PA officials whisper that the failure to hold local elections is based on the fear that Hamas might take control of too many municipalities. Ironically, though, this very conspicuous lack of democracy, combined with the well-publicized abuses of power, may be contributing to an increase in the popularity of Islamists in the PA.

The question remains as to what effect the democratically elected PLC would have on the peace process if it were permitted or encouraged to have a more influential role in Palestinian governance. What would happen if the PLC took on a higher profile or a more important role in the peace process? Would strengthened democracy in the PA necessarily come at the expense of progress in improved Israeli–Palestinian relations?

The PLC's preoccupation with peace process issues like Jerusalem, prisoners, settlements, and refugees has occasionally proven an added complication to these relations. Sometimes, PLC actions vis-à-vis Israel echo those of Arafat; at other times, however, the PLC's legislative initiatives have proven to be a peace process liability. The purview of the PLC, according to provisions of existing agreements between the Palestinians and the Israelis, has been limited—officially, at least—to domestic issues. Presumably, after the interim period ends and the Palestinians achieve statehood, the scope of issues covered by the PLC will expand to include foreign relations. Yet, given the opportunity and the requisite power, the PLC would on balance probably be better for Palestinian governance and no worse for the peace process than the current system headed by Arafat. Indeed, it seems almost intuitive that better internal Palestinian governance will result in a more reliable peace partner for Israel.

Based on the fact that the PLC takes what could be described as a less conciliatory, less "pragmatic," more ideological line than Ra'is Arafat on peace-process issues, it is reasonable to assume that if the PLC played a more efficacious role in Palestinian politics, some of its hardline positions could have a detrimental short-term effect on progress in the peace process. At the same time, however, there is little doubt that a strong PLC could contribute to more transparent Palestinian governance, which in turn would make the PA a more attractive place for investment, boosting Palestinian economic prospects. In the long run, this more accountable PA would likely prove to be the more stable "peace partner." A more secure and economically prosperous Palestinian entity is more likely to make the type of concessions that will make a lasting peace with Israel possible. And finally, although there are exceptions, the axiom that democracies are less likely to wage war on each other than are other forms of government might also bode well for the future sustainability of an Israeli–Palestinian peace.

Notes

1. Like the Palestinians, Israelis also consider the PLC and democracy in the PA to be a sensitive topic. As such, the Israeli officials cited in this section preferred that their comments not be for attribution.

2. Based on author's off-the-record discussions with Oslo participants.

3. "Twenty PA Institutions, Including 11 'Ministries,' Operate Illegally in Jerusalem," Israel Ministry of Foreign Affairs Website, http://www.israel.org/mfa/, September 9, 1998. Even after the election of Prime Minister Ehud Barak, the Website continued to condemn PLC activities in Jerusalem as violations of the Oslo accords.

4. *Qanun al-Difa'a al-Madani* [The Civil Defense Law], May 28, 1998, available on the PLC Website, http://www.pal-plc.org. Among other things, the Civil Defense Law establishes formal PA procedures for coping with "air raids."

5. Joel Singer, "The Emerging Palestinian Democracy under the West Bank and Gaza Strip Self-Governing Arrangements," *1997 Israel Yearbook on Human Rights* 26 (Zoetermeer, Netherlands: Martinus Nijhoff, 1997), pp. 313–365.

6. Robert Pelletreau, then-assistant secretary of state for Near Eastern affairs, before the U.S. Interreligious Committee for Peace in the Middle East, New York, N.Y., January 3, 1996.

7. See "Indyk: Democracy in the Arab World is not a Prerequisite for Peace," *Ha'aretz* (in Hebrew), July 18, 1996.

8. Secretary of State Warren Christopher, White House Press Briefing, July 15, 1994, online at http://www.pub.whitehouse.gov.

9. "Remarks by the President to the AIPAC Policy Conference," Washington Sheraton Hotel, Washington, May 7, 1995, online at http://www.pub.whitehouse.gov. In his speech, Clinton also included "confronting terror" as a necessary element for peace to succeed. Three years earlier, Clinton wrote, "Our foreign policy must promote democracy and stability. . ."; see William Clinton, *Putting People First* (New York: Times Books, 1992).

10. Nicholas Burns, State Department briefing, January 4, 1996, online at http://secretary.state.gov.

11. "Secretary of State Madeleine Albright Radio Address to the Palestinian People on the *Voice of Palestine*, Ramallah," September 12, 1997, online at http://secretary.state.gov.

12. U.S. Consul General Edward Abington's remarks during a USAID–Palestinian Legislative Council grant ceremony in Gaza, February 4, 1997, online at http://www.usis-israel.org.il.

13. Ibid.

14. "Remarks by the President to the Members of the Palestinian National Council and Other Palestinian Organizations," made in Gaza City, Gaza; available online at http://www.usia.gov.

15. On September 4, 1999, for example, Albright thanked Arafat and praised him for his role in coming to an agreement with Barak on the Sharm al-Shaykh Memorandum. The text of the letter was published in *al-Ayyam*; see Abd al-Rauf Arnawat, "La rabt bayna al-insihab wa 'itifaq al-'itar" [There is No Connection between the Withdrawal and the Agreement on the Framework], *al-Ayyam*, September 7, 1999, online in Arabic at http://www.al-ayyam.com.

16. These violations are detailed in "The Occupied Territories Country Report on Human Rights Practices for 1998," U.S. Department of State, Bureau of Democracy, Human Rights, and Labor, online at http://www.state.gov.

17. Testimony of Martin Indyk, assistant secretary of state for Near Eastern affairs, before the U.S. House of Representatives International Relations Committee, June 8, 1999.

18. "Washington tad'u Amman li-fath hewar ma' al-Rajoub" [Washington Calls for Amman to Open a Dialogue with Rajoub], *al-Sharq al-Awsat* online (in Arabic), July 22, 1999, at http://www.alsharqalawsat.com.

19. Lisa Anderson, "Peace and Democracy in the Middle East: The Constraints of Soft Budgets," *Journal of International Affairs* 49 (Summer 1995), pp. 25–44.

20. General Accounting Office, "Assistance for the West Bank and Gaza Strip" (GAO/NSAAID-98-85R), February 18, 1998. "Obligations" refer to the amount of money allocated to a particular project or funding area.

21. *USAID FY2000 Congressional Presentation*, online at http://gopher.info.usaid.gov/pubs/. The substantial increase may reflect a few new West Bank/Gaza USAID projects, including a community services program and a project focused on development of the judiciary. This request represents 17 percent of USAID's total congressional request for Fiscal Year 2000 for the West Bank and Gaza.

22. "Democracy and governance" is one of three USAID strategic objectives in the West Bank and Gaza. The other two are providing additional economic opportunities and increasing water resources.

23. An additional USAID contractor, the National Democratic Institute (NDI) received approximately 15 percent of the total USAID budget for democratization in the PA.

24. General Accounting Office, "U.S. Assistance for the West Bank and Gaza Strip" (GAO/NSAAID-98-85R), February 18, 1998.

25. In addition to its work with CPRS, the International Republican Institute (IRI) also worked extensively (and continues to provide support) to the Health, Development, Information, and Policy Institute (HDIP), another Palestinian NGO.

26. NDI conducted a series of workshops with PLC members and legislators from around the world to provide Palestinian legislators with a

broad perspective of how parliamentary democracy should work. In 1998, NDI also published a training manual as part of its work on civil society, entitled *Kayfiyyat 'Injaz al-Mahamat* [How to Accomplish Tasks], which included a detailed chapter on how most effectively to lobby the PLC.

27. Respectively, these documents are *Mulahathat 'ama mukhtasara 'ala mashru' qanun al-sulta al-qada'iyya* [Brief General Notes on the Draft Judiciary Law] and *Muqarana li-aham murtakazat qanun istiqlal al-qada'* [A Comparison of the Most Important Themes of Laws of Judicial Independence]. The judiciary law, passed by the PLC in December 1998, still awaits Arafat's ratification.

28. *USAID RFP (Request for Proposal) #294-99-012*, p. 8, online at http://www.info.usaid.gov.

29. ARD's expanded scope of work entails working with the *Diwan al Fatwa wa-al-Tashre'i*—the legislative drafting unit in the Ministry of Justice—to create a more uniform style of drafting legislation in the PA.

30. "Performance Measurement Report no. 2," (draft) submitted to USAID/West Bank and Gaza, by ARD, December 31, 1998.

Chapter 7

CONCLUSION

"Sure, we have political and economic problems with Israel, but our institutions are nothing more than decor; power is in the hands of one man and there is no law and order."

—Ali Jarbawi, professor of political science, Bir Zeit University[1]

In many ways, the development of the Palestinian Legislative Council (PLC) since 1996 is representative of the evolution of Palestinian governance. Four years after its inaugural election, the legislature—like the Palestinian Authority (PA) itself—remains a work in progress. Structurally, the PLC has grown to resemble a Western-style parliament. Yet, despite some great achievements, the PLC's ability to enact legislation and ensure the accountability of the executive authority remains limited. As it has evolved, the PLC and its relative position vis-à-vis the executive authority are not what the Palestinian–Israeli Interim Agreement on the West Bank and the Gaza Strip (Oslo II) envisioned and meticulously diagrammed. Indeed, Oslo II stated, "All Palestinian people in the West Bank and Gaza Strip will be all accountable to the Palestinian [Legislative] Council."[2] Perhaps because the PLC was not established until two years after Yasir Arafat arrived in Gaza, or possibly because of Arafat's revolutionary credentials, the legislature has been unable to assume a significant role. Whatever the reason, powers originally assigned to the PLC devolved to Arafat—the *ra'is* (president)—leaving the legislature emasculated.

Nonetheless, the PLC has gone about its duties, legislating and attempting to monitor and provide oversight to the executive. PLC efforts in these areas have had mixed results.

Oversight of the executive authority has been insufficient, and legislation—although sometimes ratified—has seldom been implemented. PLC members are aware of the problems facing their institution, but unfortunately, most legislators do not perceive the PLC's relative lack of power as a problem.

Systemic imbalances and a largely coopted membership have enabled Arafat and the executive authority to ignore the legislature with impunity, rendering PLC legislative and monitoring efforts largely irrelevant. Since its establishment, the PLC has squandered what few opportunities arose to exert legislative will. Despite the publication of the PLC's 1997 Corruption Report, PLC members subsequently voted their confidence in a "reconstituted" Arafat government that included all the members previously cited for corruption. Even the extremely compelling case of corruption could not persuade the PLC to override executive will. Many Palestinians gave up hope in the PLC following this incident. The Corruption Report episode is indicative of the extent to which the executive authority has PLC members under its control. Implications of PLC inaction in the aftermath of the report have not gone unnoticed. Ghassan Shakah, a prominent Palestinian politician and close confidant of Arafat, did not mince words when he described the problem. "If the PLC was serious," he said, " it would use its vote of no confidence."[3]

Three years of executive authority abuses have left the few remaining committed legislators disheartened, frustrated, and angry. This has been compounded by some incidents of gratuitous executive authority disrespect for PLC parliamentary immunity. Being ignored, abused, and ineffective has also encouraged apathy in the legislature. Despite a heightened level of legislative activism in its first few years (1996–98), year three (1998–99) witnessed a decline in activity and a marked decrease in legislative productivity. Given the current situation in the PA, one would expect this trend to continue. The only potential solution to the anemic nature of the PLC may be to hold new elections, bring in a new cadre of motivated legislators, and reinvigorate the institution.

As the PA moves toward statehood, democratic institutions are becoming increasingly important. If and when new elections are held, the Palestinian Legislative Council could eventually play a key role in PA politics. Its initial four years, however, were years of desperate struggle for the PLC. The current system of Palestinian governance—in which the executive undermines the authority and credibility of the PLC at every turn—will continue to prevent the PLC from realizing its potential. In March 1999, Ibrahim Abu al-Naja, the PLC's first deputy Speaker, boasted of the previous year's accomplishments, saying that the PLC had "managed to realize important steps, especially in the scope of ratifying laws."[4] Although the PLC has made impressive strides in its legislative endeavors, passing laws constitutes only a small fraction of what an effective legislature should do. In most of its other important functions, the PLC faced endless obstructions. Until fundamental systemic changes are made in the PA, the PLC will, unfortunately, continue to be democratic window dressing for an authoritarian government.

Policy Recommendations

Legislatures in authoritarian states are situated in inherently precarious positions. Impotent, coopted, and sometimes corrupt, these institutions are routinely dismissed as rubber stamps to legitimize dictators. Despite acknowledged operational inefficiencies of these parliaments, however, they often do serve an important role within the societies in which they exist. To some extent, by going through the motions of democratic parliamentary procedure, legislatures act as mechanisms of change. They debate taboo topics, alert the citizenry to ongoing key issues, and provide exposure to democratic ideals. Also, by contending with the mundane day-to-day matters of government, legislatures can encourage a shift from ideological to more procedural concerns of statehood.[5] In short, legislatures—impotent or otherwise—can stimulate democracy. Although the PA has not yet attained statehood, the PLC is no exception to the points mentioned above.

In the Middle East, U.S. expectations for good governance are low. Yet, because of the Palestinians' high level of education, advanced civil society, and intimate knowledge of and respect for Israeli democracy, U.S. and Palestinian expectations were unusually high when the Palestinians began to rule themselves in 1994. At the time, it was hoped that the PA would become the first full-fledged Arab democracy. Despite these hopes, the concept of democracy remains a "completely new phenomenon" for Palestinians—at least according to one USAID evaluation.[6] Given this reality, it is perhaps not surprising that, since its establishment, the PA has been beset by democratic underdevelopment. Washington's neutral disposition toward the PLC and other Palestinian democrats has not helped matters.

The U.S. policy of ignoring the PLC and other democratic elements in the PA is unfair to Palestinians and counterproductive to long-term U.S. policy goals of peace, stability, and democracy in the Middle East. Joshua Muravchik's 1993 U.S. policy prescription for the Middle East is instructive here. "Overall," he wrote, "our main task must be to nurture democratic forces in undemocratic countries."[7] In the PA, this necessarily means supporting the development of the Palestinian Legislative Council.

A more effective U.S. policy regarding the PLC might entail, among other things, the following:

(1) **A concerted U.S. effort to establish and maintain high-level contacts with the legislature.** U.S. officials have periodically reached out to the PLC, but there has been no attempt to systematize this type of activity.[8] Outreach could be facilitated through the establishment via Congress of caucus relationships, monitoring commissions, or even a permanent congressional liaison to the PLC. The framework of these mechanisms are neither difficult to establish nor particularly expensive to fund. In a similar vein, the current level of two-way exchanges between the American and Palestinian assemblies could be increased, strengthening the personal and professional ties between American and Palestinian legislators. These exchanges currently include frequent training of PLC legislators and committee personnel in various state legislatures throughout the United States. An institutionalized relationship could provide

the United States with more leverage to encourage the PLC to pass better laws—ones that are consistent with PA commitments. The United States did this in May 1997, when the Department of State denounced the PA policy regarding land sales to Jews as "very disturbing." This comment should have also been directed, at a later date, toward the PLC—which started to legislate this de facto PA policy in June 1997.

(2) **Encouragement for Palestinian democracy and transparent governance.** In addition to establishing ongoing high level contacts between the U.S. government and the PLC, it is incumbent that Washington begin to send a consistent message that democratization is a policy priority that will be supported. Many Palestinian democrats—both inside the PLC and in the NGO community—feel isolated and abandoned by the United States. The United States must encourage the nascent Palestinian democracy. In December 1998, when President Clinton addressed a special session of the Palestinian National Council and the PLC in Gaza, he mentioned nothing about democracy or good governance. The absence of a real and stated commitment to these principles at the top levels of the U.S. government sends a message to Palestinians. An ambiguous U.S. position on Palestinian democracy only encourages the PA executive to continue its abuse of the already weak and vulnerable PLC.

(3) **Encouragement of Palestinian elections.** The United States—and President Bill Clinton—have high standing among Palestinians. Washington should capitalize on its unique position to encourage ongoing democratic processes in the PA—particularly elections, both parliamentary and local. The last elections held in the PA (for the legislature and the presidency) were held in January 1996. No election has been held for the vacant Gaza City seat of Haidar Abdel Shafi, who resigned from the PLC in 1997; local elections have never been held and are not on the agenda. Without elections, there is no real sense of accountability to the constituencies, either among the current slate of legislators or among the Arafat-appointed mayoralties and local councils. Whereas elections themselves are not "democracy," they would

encourage a more vibrant democratic environment in the PA. Elections would also cause Palestinians—both pro- and anti-Oslo—to have a more personal stake in the success of ongoing peace-process negotiations. Elections in the PA have been suspended until statehood has been declared. After statehood, though, another crisis in Palestinian politics could arise to justify a further postponement. The United States must make it clear that elections, be they local or national, are an essential component of good governance, and should not be unnecessarily deferred in the PA.

(4) **Support for controversial issues, such as human rights.** Until now, U.S. support for the PLC has largely focused on uncontroversial issues. In 1999, however, the U.S. government contractor ARD attempted to push ahead with two training initiatives focused on human rights and financial transparency in the PA. Political pressure from the Palestinians quickly ended these initiatives. Despite the inherent risks, the PLC consistently engages in debate and executive oversight focused on issues of human rights and financial transparency. In the future, the United States should lend its support to these types of controversial activities, with or without the approval of the ra'is and the Speaker of the PLC. In the final analysis, these are the key issues and initiatives that must be addressed to establish a real system of checks and balances and to improve the nature of Palestinian governance.

(5) **Financial support for the PLC.** Last but not least, it is imperative that the United States continue its ongoing financial support for the legislature. A strong Palestinian history of civil society does not in any way ensure a transition to a democratic Palestinian society. The roots of a nascent democratic Palestinian entity must be cultivated with the greatest care. Washington must stay engaged, ready to provide moral, technical, and material support. It should use its power and influence to nurture democratic forces in the PA. In the long run, democratization of the Palestinian Authority would benefit the Palestinians, the Israelis, and the United States.

Notes

1. Ali Jarbawi, professor of political science, Beir Zeit University, quoted in *Jordan Times,* June 23, 1999.

2. See Article I (4) in "Annex I: Protocols Concerning Redeployment and Security Arrangements," in the *Israeli–Palestinian Interim Agreement on the West Bank and Gaza Strip,* September 28, 1995, available online at the Israeli Ministry of Foreign Affairs Website, http://www.mfa.gov.il.

3. Author interview with Ghassan Shakah, February 15, 1999. In addition to being a member of the PLC, Shakah is the mayor of Nablus and a member of the PLO Executive Committee.

4. Ja'far Sadaqah, "PLC May Withdraw Confidence over Budget," *al-Ayyam,* March 16, 1999, Foreign Broadcast Information Service (FBIS)—Near East and South Asia (FBIS-NES-1999-0317), March 19, 1999.

5. Abdo Baakline, Guilain Denoeux, Robert Springborg, *Legislative Politics in the Arab World* (Boulder, Colo.: Lynne Rienner, 1999).

6. *Evaluation of Civic Education and Civic Forum in the West Bank, Gaza Strip and East Jerusalem, Report on Qualitative Research* (Vancouver, B.C.: Viewpoints Research Ltd., February 9, 1998), p. 5.

7. Joshua Muravchik, "Exporting Democracy to the Arab World," in Yehuda Mirsky and Matt Ahrens, eds., *Democracy in the Middle East: Defining the Challenge* (Washington: The Washington Institute for Near East Policy, 1993), p. 8.

8. When Consul General Edward Abington served in Jerusalem, he took an active interest in Palestinian democratization and was an overt supporter of the PLC in its struggle against Arafat. During his tenure in al-Bireh, it is said that some Palestinians referred to Abington as the "eighty-ninth member" of the PLC. In August 1999, Republican and Democratic U.S. congressional delegations visited the PLC on a trip sponsored by the American Israel Public Affairs Committee and met with top Palestinian legislators. In July 1998, a PLC delegation headed by PLC Speaker Abu Ala visited the U.S. Congress and met with then–Speaker of the House Newt Gingrich. "Wafd min al-Kongres al-'Amriki yaltaqi 'adadan min al-nuwab fi maqar al-Tashre'i b'Ramallah" [A Delegation from the American Congress Meets a Number of Members at the PLC Building in Ramallah], *al-Ayyam,* August 23, 1999, online in Arabic at http://www.al-ayyam.com.

Appendix I: PLC Candidate and Member Affiliation

Pre-Election Stated Affiliation[1]

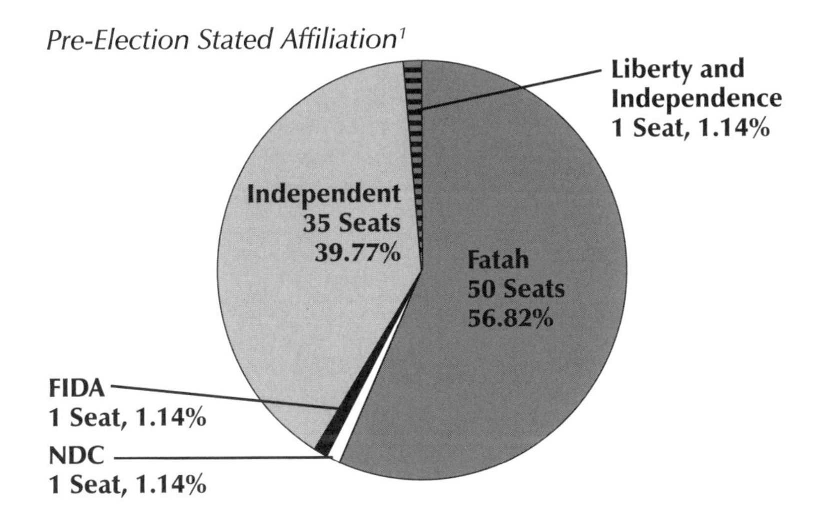

Post-Election Stated Affiliation[2]

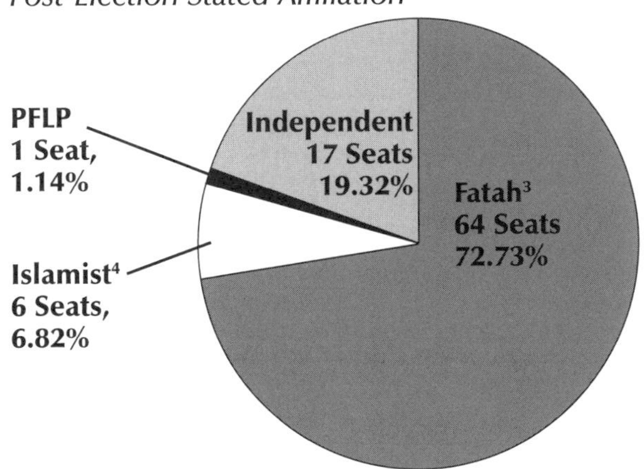

Notes:

1. Based on figures culled from "The Palestinian Council," a copublication of the Jerusalem Media and Communication Centre and the Friedrich-Ebert-Stiftung, Jerusalem.
2. Based on PLC member profiles on the official PLC Website, http://www.pal-plc.org
3. Fatah includes PLC members who describe themselves as "Fatah," "Fatah Independent," and "Fatah Revolutionary Council."
4. Islamist includes PLC members who describe themselves as "Hamas," "Close to Hamas," and "Islamist Independent."

Appendix II: Procedural Path of Draft Law (Bill) in the PLC

Adapted from a chart provided by the Associates for Rural Development; numbers in parentheses refer to articles in PLC Standing Orders

1. **Members and Committees** suggest an idea for legislation; request made through Legal Department for drafting into proper form and style. **Council of Ministers** bills drafted through Executive Department

↓

2. **Members and Committees** review bill draft; accept by signing Sponsorship and filing bill draft and notice with Chief Clerk's Office. **Council of Ministers** files bill and explanatory notes with Speaker (65A); draft law refiled by Council of Ministers from prior session (69)

↓

3. **Chief Clerk** reviews bill draft for proper form and style; assigns official bill number; creates official bill folder; copies and distributes to Members of the PLC (65 2); produces "Notice of Introduction"; makes additional copies available to public and other interested parties

↓

4. **Speaker** refers Bill to Relevant Committee (65 A)

↓

5. **Relevant Committee** hears and reports Bill back to PLC (65 A) *(Report required within 2 weeks; PLC can take up a bill without waiting for Committee's report; Chair gives 24 hrs. notice before Committee Meeting)*

→

6. **PLC** hears Committee Report (65 C); discusses General Principles (65 B); suggests Amendments *(3 days' notice of consideration)*

↓

7. **PLC** votes on advancement (65 D)

- No → Bill dies
- Yes → PLC refers Bill to Relevant Committee for Amendment based on PLC discussion of General Principles (65 E)

↓

8. **Relevant Committee** meets *(Chair gives 24 hours notice of Committee Meeting)* Hearing and Committee Action: discusses proposed amendments to Bill based on PLC discussion of general principles (65); reports Bill with recommendations to the PLC

↓

9. **Speaker** refers Bill to Legal Committee for legal opinion only (65 F) *(Legal Committee is not empowered to amend or stop the Bill)*

↓

10. **Legal Committee** reviews; Reports Bill to the PLC with legal opinion *(Chair gives 24 hrs. notice of Committee Meeting)*

↓

11. **Speaker** directs that bill be placed on PLC agenda *(gives the required 48 hours notice)*

→

12. **PLC** undertakes **First Reading of Bill:** considers Bill, article by article; considers and votes on amendments recommended by Relevant Committee; considers and votes on amendments offered by Members; votes on each article (68 1A); votes on entire Bill (68 1A)

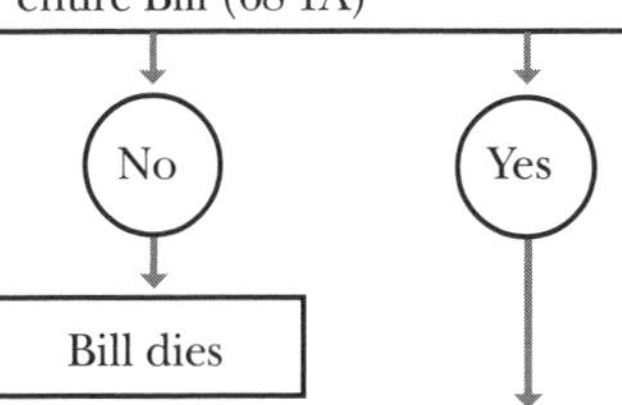

13. **Speaker** may re-refer Bill to Relevant Committee for further consideration and possible amendments if necessary (set by precedence) *(Chair gives 24 hrs. notice of Committee Meeting)* Hearing and Committee action: proposes amendments to Bill; reports Bill with recommendations to the PLC

14. **Speaker** schedules Bill under order of business within max. one month for **Second Reading of Bill** (68 1B); directs bill be placed on PLC agenda *(gives required 48 hours notice)*

15. **PLC** considers and votes on further amendments; (does not vote on each article); votes on entire Bill; requires majority vote to pass unless stated otherwise

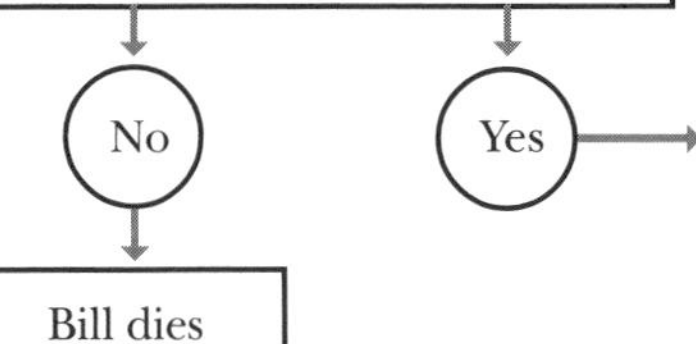

16. **Speaker** may re-refer Bill to Relevant Committee for further consideration and possible amendments, if necessary *(set by precedence; Chair gives 24 hours notice of Committee Meeting)* Hearing and Committee action: proposes amendments to the Bill; reports Bill with recommendations to the PLC

17. **Council of Ministers or 1/4 of Members** may request Bill to be rescheduled under the order of business for the **Third Reading of Bill** *(must be done within two weeks after Second Reading)* (68 2)

18. **Speaker** directs bill be placed on PLC agenda *(gives the required 48 hours notice)*

19. **PLC** undertakes **Third Reading of Bill**; considers and votes on the proposed amendments (68 2) *(does not vote on entire Bill)*

20. **President** *(within one month)* does one of the following:

approves Bill with signature (71 A) or allows it to become law without signing (71 A)	vetoes Bill and returns it, along with written objections, to PLC (71)

21. Bill becomes **Law**; is published in *Official Gazette* (70) (71 3), or...

Bill goes back to PLC; if PLC moves to override President's veto (71 A), 59 votes are needed (71 B) to repass the Bill.

Appendix III: PLC Committee Work Schedule

*Meetings held during the first period of the second session (March 8, 1998-September 2, 1998)**

Committee Name	Number of Meetings	Number of Resolutions	Number of Hearings	Field Trips
Economic	12	7	8	0
Budget and Finance	18	12	4	0
Resources and Environment	9	0	0	0
Political	14	5	0	0
Jerusalem	14	2	0	1
Refugees	13	1	0	6
Legal	12	0	0	0
Education	33	0	0	0
Land and Settlements	5	1	0	0
Oversight and Monitoring	17	3	10	0
Interior and Security	12	0	2	0
Parliamentary Affairs	6	0	0	0
TOTALS	**165**	**31**	**24**	**7**

Source: Adapted from the Arabic language chart on p. 35 of *al-Majlis al-Tashre'i Shahriyya Natiqa bi-ism al-Majlis al-Tashre'i al-Falastini* [Palestinian Legislative Council Monthly], no. 1 (1999).

Appendix IV: Translation of a PLC Resolution

Resolution 4/4/378

The PLC
in its fourth Session, first period in its fourth sitting, convened in Ramallah on Wednesday, May 12, 1999,

Taking into account
the recommendations of the Budget and Financial Affairs Committee about the future loan from the Arab Fund for Economic and Social Development.

Resolves:
The ratification of the signed agreement between the Arab Fund for Economic and Social Development and the PA which provides for a loan whose value is 3 million Kuwaiti Dinars at 3 percent interest for seventeen years with a grace period of seven years offered to the PA to implement a rural development project in Palestine.

Ahmed Qurie (Abu Ala)
Speaker of the PLC

Rawhi Fatouh
Secretary General of the PLC

Appendix V: Laws Proposed and Passed by the PLC

Number‡	Proposal	Date	Submission and Referral	General Discussion
1/96/M.*	Basic Law	5/5/96	5/8/96	7/10/96
2/96/C.M.	Election Law for the Local Councils	—	—	8/22/96
3/96/C.M.	Civil Service Law	5/8/96	5/8/96	11/7/96
4/97/C.M.	Palestinian Local Organizations	—	—	2/4/97
5/97/C.M.	General Budget '97	3/15/97	3/15/97	—
6/97/C.M.	Monetary Authority Law	5/8/96	5/8/96	3/27/97
7/97/C.	Regulating Foreigners' Ownership of Real Estate	6/16/97	6/16/97	6/16/97
8/97/C.M.	General Commission of Petroleum and Minerals	4/19/97	—	7/15/97
9/97/C.	Bar Association	7/9/97	7/10/97	7/14/97 (Note 1)
10/97/C.	Budget and Financial Affairs Regulation Law	4/30/97	3/19/98	3/19/98
11/97/C.M.	Livestock Protection Law	4/11/97	9/30/97	10/13/97
12/97/C.M.	Political Parties	1/24/97	9/30/97	11/10/97
13/97/C.	Rehabilitation and Correction Centers	11/2/97	—	11/25/97
14/97/C.	Judiciary Law	6/8/97	—	11/12/97
15/97/C.M.	Local Organizations Development Bank	4/11/97	9/30/97	10/26/97 (note 2)
16/97/C.M.	Veterinarians Law	3/27/97	9/30/97	9/30/97 (Note 3)
17/97/C.M.	Civil Defense Law	4/11/97	9/30/97	11/25/97
18/97/C.M.	Firearms and Ammunitions Law	4/19/97	9/30/97	11/25/97
19/97/M.	Non-Government Organizations	10/13/97	10/13/97	12/9/97
20/97/M.	Investment Law	11/10/97	11/10/97	12/9/97
21/97/M.	Commercial Agencies Law	11/10/97	11/10/97	12/9/97

First Reading	Second Reading	Third Reading	Date of Referral	Date Issued	*Notes*
9/1/96	9/17/96	10/2/96	10/4/96	—	Source: PLC Parliamentary Research Unit, October 12, 1999
10/10/96	12/1/96	—	—	12/16/96	
1/29/97	6/3/97	—	6/4/97	5/28/98	
2/12/97	7/2/97	7/14/97	7/21/97	10/12/97	‡ unless otherwise noted, C.M.: submitted by Council of Ministers; M.: submitted by PLC member(s); C.: submitted by a PLC committee
5/27/97	—	—	—	5/27/97	
4/11/97	6/30/97	—	12/15/97	12/16/97	
6/30/97	9/30/97	—	10/4/97	—	
9/18/97	11/25/97	—	12/7/97	—	
12/1/98	1/6/99	4/6/99	4/19/99	6/24/99	* submitted by the minister of justice
4/2/98	4/14/98	—	4/20/98	8/3/98	Note 1: postponed until 7/28/98
10/14/97	12/10/97	—	3/9/98	11/2/98	
—	—	—	—	—	Note 2: postponed pending the passage of the banks law
4/2/98	4/28/98	—	5/2/98	5/28/98	
6/25/98	9/2/98	11/25/98	12/5/98	—	Note 3: postponed pending the passage of the general syndicate law
—	—	—	—	—	
—	—	—	—	—	
1/8/98	3/31/98	—	4/20/98	5/28/98	
1/7/98	4/2/98	—	4/20/98	5/20/98	
5/30/98	7/30/98	5/25/99	8/12/99	—	
3/19/98	4/14/98	—	4/20/98	4/23/98	
1/7/99	4/20/99	6/24/99	7/15/99	—	

Number	Proposal	Date	Submission and Referral	General Discussion
22/97/C.M.	Establishment of the Palestinian Rural Development Center	4/19/97	9/30/97	8/18/98 (Note 4)
23/97/M.	Support Families of Martyrs, Prisoners of War, and Injured	—	9/30/97	7/28/98
24/97/C.M.	Public Gathering Law	3/27/97	9/30/97	4/28/98
25/97/C.M.	Jewelry Monitoring and Hallmarking	3/17/97	9/30/97	11/25/97
26/97/C.M.	Mayor's Appointment Law	4/11/97	—	7/2/97 (Note 6)
27/97/C.M.	Natural Resources Protection Law in Gaza	4/19/97	9/30/97	9/30/97 (Note 7)
28/97/M.	National Service	8/31/97	3/19/98	5/27/98
29/97/C.M.	Quotations and Tendering Regulations	7/13/97	3/19/98	5/27/98 (Note 8)
29/1-97/C.M.	Public Procurement Law	7/13/97	3/19/98	5/27/98
29/2-97/C.M.	Public Works Law	7/13/97	3/19/98	5/27/98
30/98/C.M.	Natural Resources (Revised)	1/24/98	3/19/98	4/28/98
31/98/C.M.	General Statistics	1/24/98	3/17/98	3/17/98
32/98/C.M.	Industrial Free Zones and Towns	1/24/98	3/17/98	3/17/98
33/98/M.	Welfare and Rehabilitation of Disabled	3/10/98	3/19/98	8/18/98 (Note 9)
34/98/C.M.	Budget 1998	1/27/98	3/31/98	4/28/98
35/98/C.M.	Civil Status Law	7/25/98	7/29/98	11/11/98
36/98/C.M.	Environment Law	5/16/98	5/17/98	8/18/98
37/98/C.M.	Palestinian Higher Education Law	5/16/98	5/17/98	5/27/98
38/98/C.	Palestinian Labor Law	3/8/98	3/10/98	5/27/98
39/98/C.	Government Health Insurance Law	5/20/98	—	5/27/98
40/98/M.	Access of Disabled to Public Places	5/24/98	—	5/27/98 (Note 12)
41/98/C.	Income Tax Law	10/18/98	10/20/98	12/21/98

First Reading	Second Reading	Third Reading	Date of Referral	Date Issued	*Notes*
—	—	—	—	—	Note 4: returned to Executive Authority
8/19/98 (Note 5)	—	—	—	—	Note 5: returned to committee
8/20/98	11/25/98	—	12/19/98	12/28/98	
12/9/97	3/17/98	—	3/24/98	5/28/98	Note 6: rejected
—	—	—	—	—	Note 7: returned to executive
—	—	—	—	—	Note 8: divided in two—Public Procurement, and Public Separate Works
—	—	—	—	—	
—	—	—	—	—	
7/14/98	8/18/98	—	9/14/98	11/2/98	Note 9: the law merged with the access of disabled to public facilities law on 11/5/98 and became the rights of disabled law
9/1/98	11/25/98	6/9/99	6/27/99	—	
8/19/98	11/5/98	—	12/5/98	1/24/99	
—	—	—	—	—	
7/29/98	8/18/98	—	9/9/98	11/2/98	
—	—	—	—	—	Note 10: 1998 Budget was ratified on 6/29/98
(Note 10)	—	—	—	—	
11/12/98	12/8/98	4/21/99	5/10/99	6/8/99	
5/27/99	7/6/99	—	8/5/99	—	Note 11: postponed to be submitted as part of the public health draft law
7/13/98	7/30/98	—	8/19/98	11/2/98	
12/24/98	—	—	—	—	
11/5/98 (Note 11)	—	—	—	—	Note 12: postponed until 11/5/98
1/6/99	3/16/99	5/25/99	6/2/99	8/9/99	
—	—	—	—	—	

Number	Proposal	Date	Submission and Referral	General Discussion
42/98/C.M.	Citrus Law	10/25/98	11/5/98	12/8/98 (Note 13)
43/98/C.M.	Banking Law	10/25/98	11/5/98	12/8/98
44/98/C.M.	Administrative Structures	11/4/98	11/10/98	12/8/98
45/98/C.M.	Rations Law	11/4/98	11/10/98	—
46/99/M.	Authors Law	3/1/99	3/16/99	—
47/99/M.	Publication Law	3/13/99	3/16/99	5/25/99 (Note 14)
48/99/C.M.	PA General Budget for 1999	4/5/99	4/5/99	6/9/99 (Note 15)
49/99/C.M.	Traffic Law	4/19/99	4/20/99	6/23/99
50/99/C.M.	Jewelry Monitoring and Hallmarking Law	4/19/99	4/20/99	—
51/99/M.	Palestinian Medical Council	4/25/99	5/11/99	5/25/99 (Note 16)
52/99/C.M.	Regulating Trade/ Handling of Agricultural Insecticides	6/16/99	6/24/99	—
53/99/C.M.	Arbitration	6/16/99	6/24/99	7/6/99
54/99/C.M.	General Budget for 1999	7/13/99	7/14/99	(Note 17)
55/99/M.	Palestinian Specifications and Standards	7/21/99	—	—
56/99/C.M.	Penalty Procedures	7/22/99	—	—
57/99/C.M.	Farmers Compensation Fund against Natural Disasters	8/3/99	—	—
58/99/C.M.	Consular Fees	8/3/99	—	—
59/99/C.M.	Water	8/31/99	—	—

First Reading	Second Reading	Third Reading	Date of Referral	Date Issued	*Notes*
—	—	—	—	—	Note 13: postponed during general discussion
—	—	—	—	—	
—	—	—	—	—	
—	—	—	—	—	Note 14: rejected during general discussion
—	—	—	—	—	
—	—	—	—	—	
—	—	—	—	—	Note 15: Arafat retrieved the budget
—	—	—	—	—	
—	—	—	—	—	Note 16: postponed
—	—	—	—	—	Note 17: 1999 Budget was ratified on 8/12/99
—	—	—	—	—	
—	—	—	—	—	
—	—	—	9/4/99	—	
—	—	—	—	—	
—	—	—	—	—	
—	—	—	—	—	
—	—	—	—	—	
—	—	—	—	—	

Appendix VI: Memorandum of Understanding

United States Agency for
International Development
West Bank and Gaza Mission

September 1, 1999

The Honorable Ahmed Qurie
Speaker
Palestinian Legislative Council
Ramallah

Dear Mr. Speaker,

The purpose of this letter is to set forth understandings between the United States Agency for International Development (USAID) and the Palestinian Legislative Council (the Council) as to the roles and responsibilities of the parties, as well as coordination with other Palestinian entities, during the conduct of the second phase of USAID's program with the Council. This letter is prepared in both English and Arabic. In the event of ambiguity or conflict between the two versions, the English language version will control.

Program Goal/Scope

The goal of this three-year Program is to strengthen the capability of the Palestinian Legislative Council to perform functions of a legislative body, focusing on the Council's administrative and institutional development, its legislative/deliberative and representative capacities and its relationship with the executive branch of the Palestinian Authority. The activities carried out under this program are expected to address the second generation of issues in the Council's development as a functioning legislature, with a greater emphasis on the Council's internal administration and staff capacity, establishing institutional relationships with the Executive and other bodies, and increasing the Council's public outreach.

In addition to the program described in this letter, USAID and the Council also have discussed the possibility of providing additional support for the construction or renovation of Council facilities. USAID will consider these requests in the context of this program's overall goal and the legal constraints on USAID assistance.

Program Elements

The following description of the program elements presents a general guideline for USAID's assistance to the Council over the next three years. It is designed to include the major areas where the Council is likely to require support during this timeframe. The implementation of specific programs is expected to be phased during the three year period in accordance with the Council's needs, the general operating environment and with agreements reached between USAID and the Council. The exact sequencing and relative priority of program elements will be jointly determined by USAID and the Council, and is expected to be adjusted periodically during the course of program implementation.

This program is expected to focus on strengthening the Council's capacity in the following four areas:

A. **Strengthening the Council's general administrative and institutional capacity,** through establishing administrative procedures in the areas of budgeting, procurement, public relations and personnel, and providing comprehensive training for Council administrative staff;

B. **Enhancing the Council's legislative and deliberative capacity,** through clarifying the overall legislative process, increasing access to information and expertise, and developing legislative drafting and review skills. The timing and the specific nature of this assistance will be determined in close consultation with the Council;

C. **Development of Executive/Council relations,** through establishing mechanisms for the Executive budget and expenditure review process, institutionalizing Council committee and Executive Ministry relationships and developing Council Member and staff capacity to monitor, analyze and review executive performance. The assistance in this area will be closely coordinated with the Council and with the Ministry of Parliamentary Affairs, and;

D. **Increasing interaction with constituents,** through increasing outreach and dissemination of information, and training Members and staff on how to relate to the public and the media. The timing and specific nature of this assistance will be determined in close consultation with the Council. Assistance to improve the functioning of constituency offices will be determined based on Council's decisions about the status of these offices.

Procurement Procedures and Timeframe

To carry out USAID's proposed program with the Council, USAID will conduct a full and open competition among U.S. organizations who will submit proposals to provide the services described above, subject to adjustments by USAID. USAID will form a technical review committee, comprised of representatives from USAID, to evaluate and rank all proposals. USAID will make the final selection of the contractor. USAID anticipates awarding a contract to the firm that is selected by the end of September 1999, with program implementation expected to begin in October 1999. USAID's legal obligations under this program will be contained in any such contract negotiated and signed by the USAID Contracts Officer. Nothing herein shall constitute a legally binding obligation or commitment of the U.S. Government.

USAID Responsibilities

Subject to the availability of funds, through the contractor that is selected to implement the program, USAID expects to provide training, technical assistance and material assistance to meet the program objectives over a three year period. The contractor selected by USAID will be expected to draw on local and regional sources of expertise to the maximum extent possible and to provide assistance directly in Arabic whenever feasible. The contractor will develop annual work plans for program implementation, which will be submitted to the Council and USAID for review and approval.

USAID will closely coordinate the assistance that is provided under this program and through the contractor with the Council's Liaison Committee to ensure that it directly meets the Council's needs in a timely manner. USAID and the Council will formally review program performance on at least a quarterly basis to ensure that the program is proceeding satisfactorily. USAID and the Council will use these reviews to identify and correct any issues affecting program implementation, to agree on program priorities, and to review overall achievements under the program in accordance with the established work plan of the contractor.

Council Responsibilities

The Council will be responsible for the following, as needed and appropriate, to ensure the accomplishment of program objectives:

—the provision of required Council staff to support program implementation in a timely manner;

—the designation of specific Member and staff counterparts for detailed coordination of' activities where required;

—operating expenses for staffing and functions located within the Council structure; and

—determination of those activities within the contractor's work plan that would require specific Council review and approval before implementation and a decision on the mechanism to be used to receive approval.

Commodities

USAID expects to procure commodities for the Council in accordance with the Program's SOW. USAID and the Council will mutually agree upon the commodities to be provided under this Program. The identification of the commodities that USAID expects to provide will generally be based upon a needs assessment performed by the contractor. Types of commodities which are likely to be provided are office equipment, office furniture, computer hardware and software, and other equipment in support of the achievement of program objectives.

The receiving organization will maintain inventory systems and records adequate to show receipt, location and use of all commodities provided to them through USAID's contract. Upon request, USAID will be provided access to inspect or audit the use of these commodities, which must be used to support the program objectives described above, subject to refund or return to USAID for non-compliance.

Vehicles, office equipment and other commodities to be managed by the contractor during the Program will be turned over to the Council—or other entity as mutually agreed to by the Council and USAID—upon completion of the contract, for continued use in furtherance of program objectives.

Authorized Representatives

Currently, Mr. Mohammed AlMbaid is the designated principal USAID representative for all technical and operational matters related to the Program; the Council will be advised in writing of any permanent change. USAID's representative may delegate all or part of this authority to other USAID staff as appropriate. USAID's Contracting Officer is the responsible authority for all procurement matters. No increase in costs of any contract may take place without the Contracting Officer's prior approval. The Council will be represented by the Liaison Committee.

If you are in agreement with the terms of this letter, please indicate such by countersigning below.

Sincerely,
Larry Garber
Mission Director
USAID

Countersigned:
Ahmed Qurie
Speaker
Palestinian Legislative Council

Recent Publications of

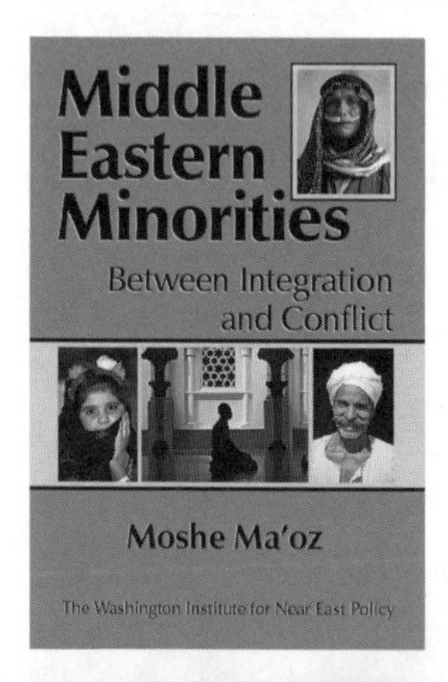

Middle Eastern Minorities: Between Integration and Conflict

Moshe Ma'oz

A broad survey of the historic and current role of religious and ethnic minorities in the Fertile Crescent, Egypt, and Sudan. Focuses on Shi'i–Sunni, Jewish–Muslim, Christian–Muslim, Kurdish–Arab, and similar relations from the mid-1800s to the present, and suggests ways that Washington policymakers can promote the political, cultural, and religious rights of minorities.

Policy Paper no. 50 (1999) ISBN 0-944029-33-7 $19.95

Crises after the Storm: An Appraisal of U.S. Air Operations in Iraq since the Persian Gulf War

Lt. Col. Paul K. White, U.S. Air Force

The second book in The Washington Institute's new series of Military Research Papers written by visiting military fellows, *Crises after the Storm* analyzes the U.S. Air Force's objectives in containing Saddam Husayn's regime in Iraq since 1991. Reviews the four main crises that have involved large-scale troop deployments to the Gulf region this decade and highlights some of the key "lessons learned" from these crises.

MRP no. 2 (1999) ISBN 0-944029-32-9 $19.95

Legal Implications of May 4, 1999

Herbert Hansell and Nicholas Rostow

Reviews the legal documents that constitute the Oslo accords and their relevance to the Israeli–Palestinian negotiations. *Policy Focus no. 37 (1999) $9.95*

The Washington Institute

Who Rules Iran? The Structure of Power in the Islamic Republic

Wilfried Buchta

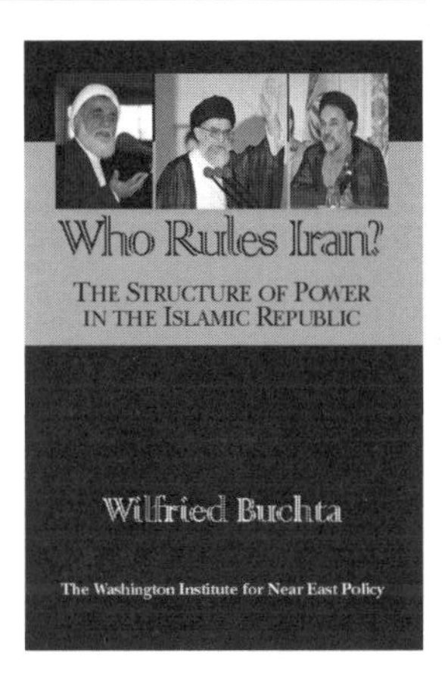

An in-depth study of the formal and informal power structures in the Islamic Republic of Iran twenty years after the 1979 Islamic Revolution. Analyzes the current religious–political dual-power relationship in Iran, prospects for its evolution, and what the sharing of power between theocrats and technocrats means for the country's future stability. Examines the ideological currents among Iran's leadership elite, as well as the various factions and branches of Iran's political system.

Monograph (1999) ISBN 0-944029-36-1
$19.95

Israeli Preconditions for Palestinian Statehood

Ze'ev Schiff

A detailed look at Israel's requirements as it enters "final-status" negotiations with the Palestinian Authority, written by the military editor of the Israeli newspaper *Ha'aretz*.

Policy Focus no. 39 (1999), $9.95

From Hussein to Abdullah: Jordan in Transition

Robert Satloff

The first comprehensive assessment of the changes taking place in Jordan under King Abdullah II. Examines domestic issues such as economic reform, as well as foreign policy issues.

Policy Focus no. 38 (1999) $9.95